CHRISTIANITY AND OTHER RELIGIONS

CHRISTIANITY AND OTHER RELIGIONS

Selected Readings

edited by
John Hick and Brian Hebblethwaite

FORTRESS PRESS Philadelphia

First published in Great Britain by Fount Paperbacks, William Collins Sons, Ltd., in 1980

First Fortress Press edition 1981

Library of Congress Cataloging in Publication Data
Main entry under title:

Christianity and other religions.

Bibliography: p.
Includes index.
CONTENTS: Troeltsch, E. The place of Christianity among the world religions.—Barth, K. The revelation of God as the abolition of religion.—Rahner, K. Christianity and the non-Christian religions.—[etc.]
1. Christianity and other religions—Addresses, essays, lectures. I. Hick, John. II. Hebblethwaite Brian.
BR127.C474 1981 261.2 80-2383
ISBN 0-8006-1444-5

8573G80 Printed in the United States of America 1-1444

CONTENTS

INTRODUCTION

The relation between Christianity and other religions has become one of the most pressing themes for Christian self-understanding today. It is impossible for Christians to ignore the existence of other flourishing world faiths which provide spiritual homes for hundreds of millions of people. And as for the missionary enterprise of the Christian churches, the collapse of Western colonialism and the loss of Western self-confidence have only reinforced the need for drastic reappraisal already imposed on the churches by their relative failure to make much headway in Asia and the Middle East. The small indigenous churches in the non-Christian lands are also having to re-think their attitudes to the majority faiths around them.

A number of different reactions to these problems, from both Catholic and Protestant sources, are illustrated in this collection of readings. For the most part, the authors are theologians, concerned to stand back from the primary tasks of the churches and to reflect on the implications of the fact that, after nearly two thousand years, Christianity still finds itself to be one of a number of vital and thriving world faiths. But we have also included selections illustrating more immediate and practical involvement with men and women of other faiths, and one major church statement, the declaration by the Second Vatican Council (1965) on the relationship of the Church to non-Christian religions.

The selected readings are given here in chronological order. This indicates at once an important fact about the spectrum of Christian attitudes to other religions. There is in no sense a linear development from traditional to radical attitudes. On the contrary the earliest paper included in this collection, that of the German theologian and sociologist, Ernst Troeltsch, represents the most radical viewpoint of all, with the possible exception of that of my co-editor, Professor John Hick of Birmingham University. The position which they exemplify can be characterized as the affirmation of religious pluralism. Christians must cease to think of their faith as bearing witness to God's final and absolute self-revelation to man. Rather they must learn to recognize their experience of God in Christ to be but one of many different saving encounters with the divine which have been given to different historical and cultural segments of mankind.

At the other end of the spectrum, there is the massive figure of Karl Barth, arguably the greatest theologian of the modern period, presenting an uncompromising view of God's self-revelation in Jesus Christ over against all religious experience and aspiration, including those of the Christian.

Closer to the 'religious pluralist' than to the 'Christian absolutist' end of the spectrum stand the figures of Paul Tillich and Wilfred Cantwell Smith. Tillich's theory of religious symbolism may seem to open the way to theological pluralism, and he certainly wishes to recognize the presence of the Spirit in the depths of every living faith. Yet there remains in Tillich the conviction that the figure of Christ provides a symbol 'which stands for the *decisive* self-manifestation in human history of the source and aim of all being' (my italics). Cantwell Smith argues effectively against doctrinal exclusivism, and indeed attempts to play down the significance of doctrine as such. Yet one may well think that his moral universalism still has specifically Christian doctrinal implications.

The remaining selections fall, more clearly and explicitly, somewhere in between the extremes of 'religious pluralism' and 'Christian absolutism'. Of particular interest are the Roman Catholic contributions. For nothing has demonstrated more forcefully both the fact of and the necessity for a more positive attitude to other religions than the changes in outlook which the Roman Catholic Church has undergone since the Second World War. The pioneering studies of Karl Rahner introduced the controversial notion of the 'anonymous Christian', and the Second Vatican Council's declaration took pains to state the truths held in common by Christians and by men and women of other faiths. Raymond Panikkar, writing out of a particular dialogue situation in India, argues that the Christian must expect to find Christ, hidden and unknown, but present none the less in Hinduism.

The other contributions by Protestant authors explore, in different ways, the nature and conditions of genuine dialogue between Christians and men and women of other religions. Broadly speaking they combine a conviction of the finality of Christ with a recognition of the spiritual value of other faiths. One of the questions which this collection is bound to raise in readers' minds is whether it is possible to sustain an open and creative dialogue without going all the way with Troeltsch and Hick.

Brian Hebblethwaite

CAMBRIDGE, DECEMBER 1979

1. THE PLACE OF CHRISTIANITY AMONG THE WORLD RELIGIONS

Ernst Troeltsch

This lecture was written for delivery before the University of Oxford in 1923, but Troeltsch died before it could be given. After some opening remarks (omitted here), Troeltsch refers to his earlier work, The Absolute Validity of Christianity, *now reissued as* The Absoluteness of Christianity *(London, 1972).*

To put it briefly, the central meaning of this book consists in a deep and vivid realization of the clash between historical reflection and the determination of standards of truth and value. The problem thus arising presented itself to me at a very early age. I had had a predominantly humanistic and historical education, from which I had been led to extend my studies and interests over a wide field of historical investigation, using the terms 'history' and 'humanity' in the sense we in Germany have been wont to attribute to them in our best periods – namely, in the objective sense of a contemplation of objects which covers as far as possible the whole extent of human existence, and which finds its delight in all the abundant diversity and ceaseless movement characteristic of human existence, and this without seeking any precise practical ends. It seems to us that it is the wealth of moral life and development that manifests itself in this endlessly diversified world of history, and imparts some of its own loftiness and solemnity to the soul of the observer.

I was, however, inspired by another interest, which was quite as strong and quite as much a part of my natural endowment as the first, I mean the interest in reaching a vital and effective religious position, which could alone furnish my life with a centre of reference for all practical questions, and could alone give meaning and purpose to reflection upon the things of this world. This need of mine led me to theology and philosophy, which I devoured with an equally passionate interest. I soon discovered, however, that the historical studies which had so largely formed me, and the theology and philosophy in which I was now immersed, stood in sharp opposition, indeed even in conflict, with one another. I was confronted, upon the one hand, with the perpetual flux of the historian's data, and the distrustful attitude of the historical critic towards conventional traditions, the real events of the past being, in his view, discoverable only as a reward of ceaseless toil, and then only with approximate accuracy. And, upon the other hand, I perceived the impulse in men towards a definite practical standpoint – the eagerness of the trusting soul to receive the divine revelation and to obey the divine commands. It was largely out of this conflict, which was no hypothetical one, but a fact of my own practical experience, that my entire theoretical standpoint took its rise.

Though this conflict was a personal one, however, it was no mere accident of my personal experience. It was rather the personal form in which a vital problem characteristic of the present stage of human development presented itself to me. I am of course aware that the sting of this problem is not equally felt in all parts of the civilized world of Europe and America. As Bouquet has explained in the work I have already mentioned, we must not apply without reservation to England, still less to America with its very underdeveloped historical sense, what is true, in this respect, of other countries.

Nevertheless, there exists at bottom, everywhere, an impression that historical criticism and the breadth of historical interest are fraught with danger to the recognition of simple standards of value, be they of rational or traditional origin. In the Anglo-Saxon countries it is especially ethnography and the comparative study of religion, together with careful philosophical criticism, that produce this attitude. In my own country it is primarily an examination of European civilization itself that has impressed us with the relativity and transitoriness of all things, even of the loftiest values of civilization. The effect, however, is very similar in the two cases. Whether we approach it from the standpoint of Herbert Spencer and the theory of evolution, or from that of Hegel and Ranke and German Romanticism, history presents a spectacle of bewildering diversity, and of historical institutions as all in a perpetual state of movement from within.

Indeed, the comparative study of religion, which gives an additional impulse to the tendency to relativity produced by historical reflection, has been pre-eminently the work of the great colonizing nations, especially of the English and the Dutch. And the criticism of the Bible and of dogma is not without representatives in England; and thus a growing feeling of uncertainty has been created here in this department also. The difference between this English line of reflection and the historical thought of Germany really consists simply in the fact that the latter is less wont to consider the practical needs and interests of society, whilst in theory it is determined more by the concept of individuality than by sociological or evolutionary principles which tend to regard all processes as leading to a single goal presented by nature.

Important as these differences are, however, they are

all but different aspects of the one fundamental conflict between the spirit of critical scepticism generated by the ceaseless flux and manifold contradictions within the sphere of history and the demand of the religious consciousness for certainty, for unity, and for peace. Whether this conflict becomes more apparent in the critical analysis of details or in the challenging of fundamental principles, the cause and the general effect remain very much the same.

In my book on *The Absolute Validity of Christianity* I examined the means whereby theology is able to defend itself against these difficulties. This of course involved an examination of the fundamental concepts of theology as such. I believed that I could here determine two such concepts, both of which claimed to establish the ultimate validity of the Christian revelation in opposition to the relativities revealed by the study of history.

The first of these concepts was the theory that the truth of Christianity is guaranteed by miracles. In our times we are no longer primarily concerned here with miracles in the external world, i.e. with the so-called 'nature miracles', involving an infringement of natural law, but with the miracles of interior conversion and the attainment of a higher quality of life through communion with Jesus and his community. In this connection, it is claimed, an entirely different type of causation comes into operation from that which is operative anywhere else in the world. The Christian life may indeed be compared to an island in the midst of the stream of history, exposed to all the storms of secular life, and lured by all its wiles, yet constituting, in reality, a stronghold of experience of quite another order. The absolute validity of Christianity rests upon the absoluteness of God himself, who is made manifest here directly in miracles but who manifested himself beyond this island only as a *causa remota* – as the ground of the interconnection of all relative things. In this way both a natural and a supernatural theology are possible, the latter resting upon the new birth and experience of the inner man, whilst natural theology is based upon the facts and forces of the external world. This theory is simply a restatement of the old miracle apologetic in the more intimate and spiritual form which it acquired under the influence of Methodism and Pietism.

The second fundamental concept of theology, which I have called the concept of evolution, presents a considerable contrast to the first. Its most important exponent is Hegel. According to this view Christianity is simply the perfected expression of religion as such. In the universal process of the unfolding of Spirit, the fundamental impulse towards salvation and communion with God overcomes all the limitations of sense experience, of the natural order, of mythological form, until it attains perfect expression in Christianity, and enters into combination with the loftiest and most spiritual of all philosophies, namely, that of Platonism. Christianity, it is maintained, is not *a particular* religion, it is *religion.* It is no isolated manifestation of Spirit, but the flower of spiritual life itself. All religion implies salvation and re-birth, but outside Christianity these are subject to the limitations of physical nature and are baulked by human selfishness. In the prophets and in Christ the Divine Life breaks through these limits and flows unrestrained into the thirsty world, which finds therein the solution of all its conflicts and the goal of all its striving. The whole history of religion and its obvious trend are thus a completely adequate proof of Christianity. The historical process does not stand in opposition to it. When regarded as a whole, and as one process, it rather affords a demonstration of its supreme greatness and all-embracing power. The miracles which attend its development are partly explicable, as in other religions, as mythical elements, accumulated during the growth of tradition, but they are partly effects of the shock produced by the spiritual revolution traceable here. They are thus not so much its credentials as its attendant phenomena, and as such they may be left without anxiety in the hands of the historical critic.

I found myself obliged to dismiss both these views as untenable. The former I rejected on the ground that an inward miracle, though it is indeed a powerful psychical upheaval, is not a miracle in the strict sense of the term. Are we justified in tracing the Platonic *Eros* to a natural cause, whilst we attribute a supernatural origin to the Christian *Agape*? And how can we prove such origin, even if we care to assume it? This would only be possible by having recourse once more to the visible signs which accompany these inward miracles, which would be again to treat the accompaniment as if it were itself the melody. Moreover, we should then be faced with the competition furnished by similar miracles in the non-Christian religions, not to mention the negative results of historical criticism and the trouble attendant upon every theory of miracles.

If, however, we turn for this reason to the second view, we find the difficulties to be different, indeed, but no less formidable. The actual history of religion knows nothing of the common character of all religions, or of their natural upward trend towards Christianity. It perceives a sharp distinction between the great world religions and the national religions of heathen tribes, and further discovers certain irresolvable contradictions between these world religions themselves which render their ultimate fusion and reconciliation in Christianity highly improbable, either in theory or in practice. Moreover, Christianity is itself a theoretical abstraction. It presents no historical uniformity, but displays a different character in every age, and is, besides, split up into many different denominations, hence it can in no wise be represented as the finally attained unity and explanation of all that has gone before, such as religious speculation seeks. It is rather a particular, independent, historical principle, containing, similarly to the other principles, very diverse possibilities and tendencies.

This leads us finally to a conception which has, I think, obtained less recognition in other countries than in Germany – I mean the conception which dominates the whole sphere of history, viz., Individuality. History cannot be regarded as a process in which a universal and everywhere similar principle is confined and obscured. Nor is it a continual mixing and remixing of elemental psychical powers, which indicate a general trend of things towards a rational end or goal of evolution. It is rather an immeasurable, incomparable profusion of always-new, unique, and hence individual tendencies, welling up from undiscovered depths, and coming to light in each case in unsuspected places and under different circumstances. Each process works itself out in its own way, bringing ever-new series of unique transformations in its train, until its powers are exhausted, or until it enters a component material into some new combination. Thus the universal law of history consists precisely in this, that the Divine Reason, or the Divine Life, within history, constantly manifests itself in always-new and always-peculiar individualizations – and hence that its tendency is not towards unity or universality at all, but rather towards the fulfilment of the highest potentialities of each separate department of life. It is this law which, beyond all else, makes it quite impossible to characterize Christianity as the reconciliation and goal of all the forces of history, or indeed to regard it as anything else than a historical individuality.

These are the historical ideas which have been handed down to us from German Romanticism, the great opposition movement to Rationalism and to all the clumsy miracle apologetic. They illustrate the special character and significance of German Romanticism, considered as part of the great Romantic Movement of Europe. They form the starting point of all the German history and most of the German theology of the nineteenth century. They present our problem in its most crucial form, and explain why it became a more burning problem in Germany than elsewhere, except where it was envisaged in the same way, either as a result of independent reflection or under German influence.

What, then, is the solution? This is the question which I attempted to answer in my book. I first endeavoured to show that it was in any case impossible to return to the old miracle apologetic. This has been rendered untenable, not by theories, but by documents, by discoveries, by the results of exploration. The force of such evidence cannot be resisted by anyone whose sense of truth has been educated by philology, or even by anyone possessing an average amount of ordinary 'common sense'. I then submitted that the mere fact of the universality of Christianity – of its presence in all the other religions – would, even if true – be irrelevant. The point at issue was not whether Christianity was as a matter of fact universal, or at least implicit in all religion, but whether it possessed ultimate truth, a truth which might easily depend upon a single instance of itself.

This formed a position for further reflection. It is quite possible, I maintained, that there is an element of truth in every religion, but that this is combined with innumerable transitory, individual features. This element of truth can only be disentangled through strife and disruption, and it should be our constant endeavour to assist in this process of disentanglement. The recognition of this truth is, however, an intuition which is born of deep personal experience and a pure conscientiousness. No strict proof of it is possible, for to demonstrate the actual presence of this truth in all the other cases would not be to establish its validity, even if this demonstration were easier than it is. Such an intuition can only be confirmed retrospectively and indirectly by its practical fruits, and by the light that it sheds upon all the problems of life. Thus in relation to Christianity such an intuition can only arise from immediate impression and personal conviction. Its claim to universal validity can only be felt and believed, in the first instance, and must be confirmed retrospectively through its genuine ability to furnish a solution of the various problems of life.

Now, validity of this kind seems always to rest upon the fine point of personal conviction. We still require a broader foundation upon actual, objective facts. I believed that I had discovered such a foundation for Christianity in the terms in which its claim to ultimate validity finds instinctive and immediate expression; in other words, in its faith in revelation and in the kind of claim it makes to truth. I thought it necessary to compare it from this point of view with other religions, whose belief in revelation and claim to validity were in every case of quite a different kind. If we examine any of the great world religions we shall find that all of them, Judaism, Islam, Zoroastrianism, Buddhism, Christianity, even Confucianism, indeed claim absolute validity, but quite naïvely, and that in a very different manner in each case, the differences being illustrative of differences in their inner structure. These claims are always naïve – simple and direct. They are not the outcome of an apologetic reasoning, and the differences they exhibit in their naïve claims to absolute validity indicate the varying degree of such absolute validity as they really mean and intend within their own minds. This seemed to me to be nearly the most important point in every comparison between the religions, and the one which furnished the most searching test of the character of the dogmatic contents to be compared – contents which, in themselves, reveal so little as to the manner of their foundation in immediate religious experience.

A similar line of thought is to be found in the excellent book on *National and Universal Religions*, by the Dutch writer Abraham Kuenen. If we make his distinction the basis of our investigation and comparison, we at once perceive that Judaism and Zoroastrianism were explicitly national religions, associated with a particular country and concerned with tasks presented by a particular type of civilization – in the case of the Jews primarily with questions of national loyalty and national aspiration. Islam, too, is at the bottom the national religion of the Arab peoples, compelling by the sword recognition of the prophetic claims of Mohammed in all the countries to which the Arab races have penetrated. Where, on the other hand, it has spread beyond the boundaries of Arabian territory, it has not as a rule attempted to convert unbelievers, but has simply maintained them as a source of revenue. And where Islam has developed great missionary activity, as, for example, in Africa and in the islands of the Malay Archipelago, it shows itself to be bound to certain conditions of civilization which render it more readily acceptable to primitive races than Christianity, but which prove it, at the same time, to be indissolubly connected with a particular type of civilization. Finally, where it has adopted Persian or Indian mysticism, or Greek or modern philosophy, it loses its essential character, and becomes no more than a sign and a proof of national autonomy. Confucianism and Buddhism again are rather philosophies than religions, and owe their claim to absolute validity more to the common character of thought than to belief in a specific religious revelation, whilst Confucianism is essentially a national movement and Buddhism is, as a matter of fact, bound to the conditions of life in tropical countries.

Now, the naïve claim to absolute validity made by Christianity is of quite a different kind. All limitation to a particular race or nation is excluded on principle, and this exclusion illustrates the purely human character of its religious ideal, which appeals only to the simplest, the most general, the most personal and spiritual needs of mankind. Moreover, it does not depend in any way upon human reflection or a laborious process of reasoning, but upon an overwhelming manifestation of God in the persons and lives of the great prophets. Thus it was not a theory but a life – not a social order but a power. It owes its claim to universal validity not to the correctness of its reasoning nor to the conclusiveness of its proofs, but to God's revelation of himself in human hearts and lives. Thus the naïve claim to absolute validity of Christianity is as unique as its conception of God. It is indeed a corollary of its belief in a revelation within the depths of the soul, awakening men to a new and higher quality of life, breaking down the barriers which the sense of guilt would otherwise set up, and making a final breach with the egoism obstinately centred in the individual self. It is from this point of view that its claim to absolute validity, following as it does from the content of its religious ideal, appears to be vindicated. It possesses the highest claim to universality of all the religions, for this its claim is based upon the deepest foundations, the nature of God and of man.

Hence we may simply leave aside the question of the measure of validity possessed by the other religions. Nor need we trouble ourselves with the question of the possible further development of religion itself. It suffices that Christianity is itself a developing religion, constantly striving towards a fresh and fuller expression. We may content ourselves with acknowledging that it possesses the highest degree of validity attained among all the historical religions which we are able to examine. We shall not wish to become Jews, nor Zoroastrians, nor Mohammedans, nor again Confucianists nor Buddhists. We shall rather strive continually to bring our Christianity into harmony with the changing conditions of life, and to bring its human and divine potentialities to the fullest possible fruition. It is the loftiest and most spiritual revelation we know at all. It has the highest validity. Let that suffice.

Such was the conclusion I reached in the book which I wrote some twenty years ago, and, from the practical standpoint at least, it contains nothing that I wish to withdraw. From the point of view of theory, on the other hand, there are a number of points which I should wish to modify today, and these modifications are, of course, not without some practical effects.

My scruples arise from the fact that, whilst the significance for history of the concept of Individuality impresses me more forcibly every day, I no longer believe this to be so easily reconcilable with that of supreme validity. The further investigations, especially into the history of Christianity, of which I have given the results in my *Social Doctrines* (*Die Soziallehren der christlichen Kirchen und Gruppen*, 1912), have shown me how thoroughly individual is historical Christianity after all, and how invariably its various phases and denominations have been due to varying circumstances and conditions of life. Whether you regard it as a whole or in its several forms, it is a purely historical, individual, relative phenomenon, which could, as we actually find it, only have arisen in the territory of the classical culture, and among the Latin and Germanic races. The Christianity of the Oriental peoples – the Jacobites, Nestorians, Armenians, Abyssinians – is of quite a different type, indeed even that of the Russians is a world of its own. The inference from all that is, however, that a religion, in the several forms assumed by it, always depends upon the intellectual, social, and national conditions among which it exists. On the other hand, a study of the non-Christian religions convinced me more and more that their naïve claims to absolute validity are also genuinely such. I found Buddhism and Brahminism especially to be really humane and spiritual religions, capable of appealing in precisely the same way to the inner certitude and devotion of their followers as Christianity, though the particular character of each has been determined by the historical, geographical, and social conditions of the countries in which it has taken shape.

The subject to which I devoted most attention, however, was that of the relation of individual historical facts to standards of value within the entire domain of history in connection with the development of political, social, ethical, aesthetic, and scientific ideas. I have only lately published the results of these investigations in my new book on *The Historical Temper and its Problems* (*Der Historismus und seine Probleme*), 1922. I encountered the same difficulties in each of these provinces – they were not confined to religion. Indeed, even the validity of science and logic seemed to exhibit, under different skies and upon different soil, strong individual differences present even in their deepest and innermost rudiments. What was really common to mankind, and universally valid for it, seemed, in spite of a general kinship and capacity for mutual understanding, to be at bottom exceedingly little, and to belong more to the province of material goods than to the ideal values of civilization.

The effect of these discoveries upon the conclusions reached in my earlier book was as follows.

The individual character of European civilization, and of the Christian religion which is intimately connected with it, receives now much greater emphasis, whilst the somewhat rationalistic concept of validity, and specifically of *supreme validity,* falls considerably into the background. It is impossible to deny facts or to resist the decrees of fate. And it is historical facts that have welded Christianity into the closest connection with the civilizations of Greece, Rome and Northern Europe. All our thoughts and feelings are impregnated with Christian motives and Christian presuppositions; and, conversely, our whole Christianity is indissolubly bound up with elements of the ancient and modern civilizations of Europe. From being a Jewish sect Christianity has become the religion of all Europe. It stands or falls with European civilization; whilst, on its own part, it has entirely lost its Oriental character and has become Hellenized and Westernized. Our European conceptions of personality and its eternal, divine right, and of progress towards a kingdom of the spirit and of God, our enormous capacity for expansion and for the interconnection of spiritual and temporal, our whole social order, our science, our art – all these rest, whether we know it or not, whether we like it or not, upon the basis of this deorientalized Christianity.

Its primary claim to validity is thus the fact that only through it have we become what we are, and that only in it can we preserve the religious forces that we need. Apart from it we lapse either into a self-destructive titanic attitude, or into effeminate trifling, or into crude brutality. And at the same time our life is a consistent compromise, as little unsatisfactory as we can manage, between its lofty spirituality and our practical everyday needs – a compromise that has to be renewed at every fresh ascent and every bend of the road. This tension is characteristic of our form of human life and rouses us to many a heroic endeavour, though it may also lead us into the most terrible mendacity and crime. Thus we are, and thus we shall remain, as long as we survive. We cannot live without a religion, yet the only religion that we can endure is Christianity, for Christianity has grown up with us and has become a part of our very being.

Now, obviously we cannot remain in these matters at the level of brute fact. Christianity could not be the religion of such a highly developed racial group if it did not possess a mighty spiritual power and truth; in short, if it were not, in some degree, a manifestation of the Divine Life itself. The evidence we have for this remains essentially the same, whatever may be our theory concerning absolute validity – it is the evidence of a profound inner experience. This experience is undoubtedly the criterion of its validity, but, be it noted, only of its validity *for us*. It is God's countenance as revealed to us; it is the way in which, being what we are, we receive, and react to, the revelation of God. It is binding upon us, and it brings us deliverance. It is final and unconditional for us, because we have nothing else, and because in what we have we can recognize the accents of the divine voice.

But this does not preclude the possibility that other racial groups, living under entirely different cultural conditions, may experience their contact with the Divine Life in quite a different way, and may themselves also possess a religion which has grown up with them, and from which they cannot sever themselves so long as they remain what they are. And they may quite sincerely regard this as absolutely valid for them, and give expression to this absolute validity according to the demands of their own religious feeling. We shall, of course, assume something of this kind only among nations which have reached a relatively high stage of civilization, and whose whole mental life has been intimately connected with their religion through a long period of discipline. We shall not assume it among the less developed races, where many religious cults are followed side by side, nor in the simple animism of heathen tribes, which is so monotonous in spite of its many variations. These territories are gradually conquered by the great world religions which possess a real sense of their own absolute validity. But among the great spiritual religions themselves the fundamental spiritual positions which destiny has assigned to them persist in their distinctness. If we wish to determine their relative value, it is not the religions alone that we must compare, but always only the civilizations of which the religion in each case constitutes a part incapable of severance from the rest. But who will presume to make a really final pronouncement here? Only God himself, who has determined these differences, can do that. The various racial groups can only seek to purify and enrich their experience, each within its own province and according to its own standards, and to win the weaker and less developed races for their own faith, always remembering that the religion thus adopted by another people will individualize itself anew.

The practical bearing of this new manner of thinking differs but little from that of my earlier view, or indeed from that of any theology which seeks to retain the essential basis of Christianity, and intends merely to substantiate and to interpret it. Its detailed application, however, brings to light one or two important consequences.

In the first place, it has a considerable influence upon the question of foreign missions. Missionary enterprise has always been in part simply a concomitant of the political, military, and commercial expansion of a state or nation, but in part also an outcome of the religious enthusiast's zeal for conversion. The former aspect is exceedingly important as a factor in human history, but is irrelevant in the present connection. The latter aspect, on the other hand, is intimately connected with the claim to absolute validity. But here we have to maintain, in accordance with all our conclusions hitherto, that directly religious missionary enterprise must stand in quite a different relation to the great philosophical world religions from that in which it stands to the crude heathenism of smaller tribes. There can be always only a spiritual wrestling of missionary Christianity with the other world religions, possibly a certain contact with them. The heathen races, on the other hand, are being morally and spiritually disintegrated by the contact with European civilization; hence they demand a substitute from the higher religion and culture. We have a missionary duty towards these races, and our enterprise is likely to meet with success amongst them, although Christianity, be it remembered, is by no means the only religion which is taking part in this missionary campaign. Islam and Buddhism are also missionary religions. But in relation to the great world religions we need to recognize that they are expressions of the religious consciousness corresponding to certain definite types of culture, and that it is their duty to increase in depth and purity by means of their own interior impulses, a task in which the contact with Christianity may prove helpful, to them as to us, in such processes of development from within. The great religions might indeed be described as crystallizations of the thought of great races, as these races are themselves crystallizations of the various biological and anthropological forms. There can be no conversion or transformation of one into the other, but only a measure of agreement and of mutual understanding.

The second practical consequence of my new trend of thought concerns the inner development of Christianity itself. If my theory is correct, this development is closely related to the whole spiritual and cultural development of European civilization. True, the religious consciousness, whose object is God and eternal peace, is less exposed to restlessness and change than are the purely temporal constituents of the movement; hence it has become institutionalized in the various large denominations which, because of these internal reasons, constitute the most conservative element in the life of Europe. Nevertheless, Christianity is drawn into the stream of spiritual development even within the churches, and still more outside and beyond them, in the free speculation of literature and philosophy. Moreover, it contains, like all the world religions, and perhaps more than any other world religion, the impulse and the power to a continual self-purification and self-deepening, for it has been assigned to that Spirit which shall lead men into all truth, and which seeks its fulfilment in the coming of the Kingdom of God; and again, because it has been bound up from the first with all the intellectual forces of Hellenism.

Under these circumstances the course of its development is unpredictable, for it is capable of assuming always new individualizations. A new era in the world's history is beginning for it at this moment. It has to ally itself anew to a new conception of nature, a new social order, and a profound interior transformation of the spiritual outlook, and has to bring to the suffering world a new peace and a new brotherhood. How this can be accomplished it is not for me to say here; indeed, the answer is as yet very far from clear. All that is certain is that Christianity is at a critical moment of its further development, and that very bold and far-reaching changes are necessary, transcending anything that has yet been achieved by any denomination. I have, in this respect, become more and more radical and super-denominational, whilst, at the same time, I have come more and more to regard the specific kernel of religion as a unique and independent source of life and power.

Can we, then, discover no common goal of religion, nothing at all that is absolute, in the objective sense of constituting a common standard for mankind? Instinctive conviction makes us reluctant to admit such a sceptical conclusion, and it will especially be combated on the ground of the reality of the subjective validities which we have discovered. These are not simply illusions or the products of human vanity. They are products of the impulse towards absolute objective truth, and take effect in the practical sphere under constant critical self-purification and effort at self-improvement. I have already drawn attention to this fact in my earlier work. I only wish to emphasize now more strongly than I did then that this synthesis cannot as yet be already attained in any one of the historical religions, but that they all are tending in the same direction, and that all seem impelled by an inner force to strive upward towards some unknown final height, where alone the ultimate unity and the final objective validity can lie. And, as all religion has thus a common goal in the Unknown, the Future, perchance in the Beyond, so too it has a common ground in the Divine Spirit ever pressing the finite mind onward towards further light and fuller consciousness, a Spirit which indwells the finite spirit, and whose ultimate union with it is the purpose of the whole many-sided process.

Between these two poles, however – the divine Source and the divine Goal – lie all the individual differentiations of race and civilization, and, with them also, the individual differences of the great, comprehensive religions. There may be mutual understanding between them, if they are willing to renounce those sorry things, self-will and the spirit of violent domination. If each strives to fulfil its own highest potentialities, and allows itself to be influenced therein by the similar striving of the rest, they may approach and find contact with each other. Some striking examples of such contact are recorded in Canon Streeter's *The Sadhu,* and in a book called *On the Edge of the Primeval Forest*, by the Alsatian physician and writer on the philosophy of religion, Albert Schweitzer. But, so far as human eye can penetrate into the future, it would seem probable that the great revelations to the various civilizations will remain distinct, in spite of a little shifting of their several territories at the fringes, and that the question of their several relative values will never be capable of objective determination, since every proof thereof will presuppose the special characteristics of the civilization in which it arises. The conception of personality itself is, for instance, different in the East and in the West, hence arguments starting from it will lead to different conclusions in the two cases. Yet there is no other concept which could furnish a basis for argument concerning practical values and truths save this concept of personality, which is always itself already one of the fundamental positions of the several religions, and is determined by them according to those respective general attitudes of theirs.

This is what I wish to say in modification of my former theories. I hope you feel that I am not speaking in any spirit of scepticism or uncertainty. A truth which, in the first instance, is *a truth for us* does not cease, because of this, to be very truth and life. What we learn daily through our love for our fellow men, viz., that they are independent beings with standards of their own, we ought also to be able to learn through our love for mankind as a whole – that here too there exist autonomous civilizations with standards of their own. This does not exclude rivalry, but it must be a rivalry for the attainment of interior purity and clearness of vision. If each racial group strives to develop its own highest potentialities, we may hope to come nearer to one another. This applies to the great world religions, but it also applies to the various religious denominations, and to individuals in their intercourse with one another. In our earthly experience the Divine Life is not one, but many. But to apprehend the one in the many constitutes the special character of love.

2. THE REVELATION OF GOD AS THE ABOLITION OF RELIGION

Karl Barth

The revelation of God in the outpouring of the Holy Spirit is the judging but also reconciling presence of God in the world of human religion, that is, in the realm of man's attempts to justify and to sanctify himself before a capricious and arbitrary picture of God. The Church is the locus of true religion, so far as through grace it lives by grace . . .

RELIGION AS UNBELIEF

A theological evaluation of religion and religions must be characterized primarily by the great cautiousness and charity of its assessment and judgements. It will observe and understand and take man in all seriousness as the subject of religion. But it will not be man apart from God, in a human *per se.* It will be man for whom (whether he knows it or not) Jesus Christ was born, died, and rose again. It will be man who (whether he has already heard it or not) is intended in the Word of God. It will be man who (whether he is aware of it or not) has in Christ his Lord. It will always understand religion as a vital utterance and activity of this man. It will not ascribe to this life-utterance and activity of his a unique 'nature', the so-called 'nature of religion', which it can then use as a gauge to weigh and balance one human thing against another, distinguishing the 'higher' religion from the 'lower', the 'living' from the 'decomposed', the 'ponderable' from the 'imponderable'. It will not omit to do this from carelessness or indifference towards the manifoldness with which we have to do in this human sphere, nor because a prior definition of the 'nature' of the phenomena in this sphere is either impossible or in itself irrelevant, but because what we have to know of the nature of religiòn from the standpoint of God's revelation does not allow us to make any but the most incidental use of an immanent definition of the nature of religion. It is not, then, that this 'revealed' nature of religion is not fitted in either form or content to differentiate between the good and the bad, the true and the false in the religious world. Revelation singles out the Church as the *locus* of true religion. But this does not mean that the Christian religion as such is the fulfilled nature of human religion. It does not mean that the Christian religion is the true religion, fundamentally superior to all other religions. We can never stress too much the connection between the truth of the Christian religion and the grace of revelation. We have to give particular emphasis to the fact that through grace the Church lives by grace, and to that extent it is the *locus* of true religion. And if this is so, the Church will as little boast of its 'nature', i.e. the perfection in which it fulfils the 'nature' of religion, as it can attribute that nature to other religions. We cannot differentiate and separate the Church from other religions on the basis of a general concept of the nature of religion . . .

A truly theological treatment of religion and religions, as it is demanded and possible in the Church as the *locus* of the Christian religion, will need to be distinguished from all other forms of treatment by the exercise of a very marked tolerance towards its object. Now this tolerance must not be confused with the moderation of those who actually have their own religion or religiosity, and are secretly zealous for it, but who can exercise self-control, because they have told themselves or have been told that theirs is not the only faith, that fanaticism is a bad thing, that love must always have the first and the last word. It must not be confused with the clever aloofness of the rationalistic Know-All – the typical Hegelian belongs to the same category – who thinks that he can deal comfortably and in the end successfully with all religions in the light of a concept of a perfect religion which is gradually evolving in history. But it also must not be confused with the relativism and impartiality of a historical scepticism, which does not ask about truth and untruth in the field of religious phenomena, because it thinks that truth can be known only in the form of its own doubt about all truth. That the so-called 'tolerance' of this kind is unattainable is revealed by the fact that the object, religion and religions, and therefore man, are not taken seriously, but are at bottom patronized. Tolerance in the sense of moderation, or superior knowledge, or scepticism is actually the worst form of intolerance. But the religion and religions must be treated with a tolerance which is informed by the forbearance of Christ, which derives therefore from the knowledge that by grace God has reconciled to himself godless man and his religion. It will see man carried, like an obstinate child in the arms of its mother, by what God has determined and done for his salvation in spite of his own opposition. In detail, it will neither praise nor reproach him. It will understand his situation – understand it even in the dark and terrifying perplexity of it – not because it can see any meaning in the situation as such, but because it acquires a meaning from outside, from Jesus Christ. But confronted by this object it will not display the weak or superior or weary smile of a quite inappropriate indulgence. It will see that man is caught in a way of acting that cannot be recognized as right and holy, unless it is first and at the same time recognized as thoroughly wrong and unholy. Self-evidently, this kind of tolerance, and therefore a theological consideration of religion, is possible only for those who are ready to abase themselves and their religion together with man, with every individual man, knowing that they first, and their religion, have need of tolerance, a strong forbearing tolerance.

We begin by stating that religion is unbelief. It is a concern, indeed, we must say that it is the one great concern, of godless man . . .

In the light of what we have already said, this proposition is not in any sense a negative value-judgement. It is not a judgement of religious science or philosophy based upon some prior negative judgement concerned with the nature of religion. It does not affect only other men with their religion. Above all, it affects ourselves also as adherents of the Christian religion. It formulates the judgement of divine revelation upon all religion. It can be explained and expounded, but it cannot be derived from any higher principle than revelation, nor can it be proved by any phenomenology or history of religion. Since it aims only to repeat the judgement of God, it does not involve any human renunciation of human values, and contesting of the true and the good and the beautiful which a closer inspection will reveal in almost all religions, and which we naturally expect to find in abundant measure in our own religion, if we hold to it with any conviction. What happens is simply that man is taken by God and judged and condemned by God. That means, of course, that we are struck to the very roots, to the heart. Our whole existence is called in question. But where that is the case there can be no place for sad and pitiful laments at the non-recognition of relative human greatness . . .

To realize that religion is really unbelief, we have to consider it from the standpoint of the revelation attested in Holy Scripture. There are two elements in that revelation which make it unmistakably clear.

1. Revelation is God's self-offering and self-manifestation. Revelation encounters man on the presupposition and in confirmation of the fact that man's attempts to know God from his own standpoint are wholly and entirely futile; not because of any necessity in principle, but because of a practical necessity of fact. In revelation God tells man that he is God, and that as such he is his Lord. In telling him this, revelation tells him something utterly new, something which apart from revelation he does not know and cannot tell either himself or others. It is true that he could do this, for revelation simply states the truth. If it is true that God is God and that as such he is the Lord of man, then it is also true that man is so placed towards him, that he could know him. But this is the very truth which is not available to man, before it is told him in revelation. If he really can know God this capacity rests upon the fact that he really does know him, because God has offered and manifested himself to him. The capacity, then, does not rest upon the fact, which is true enough, that man could know him. Between 'he could' and 'he can' there lies the absolute decisive 'he cannot', which can be removed and turned into its opposite only by revelation. The truth that God is God and our Lord, and the further truth that we could know him as God and Lord, can only come to us through the truth itself. This 'coming to us' of the truth is revelation. It does not reach us in a neutral condition, but in an action which stands to it, as the coming of truth, in a very definite, indeed a determinate relationship. That is to say, it reaches us as religious men; i.e. it reaches us in the attempt to know God from our standpoint. It does

not reach us, therefore, in the activity which corresponds to it. The activity which corresponds to revelation would have to be faith; the recognition of the self-offering and self-manifestation of God. We need to see that in view of God all our activity is in vain even in the best life; i.e. that of ourselves we are not in a position to apprehend the truth, to let God be God and our Lord. We need to renounce all attempts even to try to apprehend this truth. We need to be ready and resolved simply to let the truth be told us, and therefore to be apprehended by it. But that is the very thing for which we are not resolved and ready. The man to whom the truth has really come will concede that he was not at all ready and resolved to let it speak to him. The genuine believer will not say that he came to faith from faith, but – from unbelief, even though the attitude and activity with which he met revelation, and still meets it, is religion. For in faith, man's religion as such is shown by revelation to be resistance to it. From the standpoint of revelation religion is clearly seen to be a human attempt to anticipate what God in his revelation wills to do and does do. It is the attempted replacement of the divine work by a human manufacture. The divine reality offered and manifested to us in revelation is replaced by a concept of God arbitrarily and wilfully evolved by man . . .

'Arbitrarily and wilfully' means here by his own means, by his own human insight and constructiveness and energy. Many different images of God can be formed once we have engaged in this undertaking, but their significance is always the same . . .

The image of God is always that reality of perception or thought in which man assumes and asserts something unique and ultimate and decisive either beyond or within his own existence, by which he believes himself to be posited or at least determined and conditioned. From the standpoint of revelation, man's religion is simply an assumption and assertion of this kind, and as such it is an activity which contradicts revelation – contradicts it, because it is only through truth that truth can come to man. If a man tries to grasp at truth of himself he tries to grasp at it *a priori*. But in that case he does not do what he has to do when the truth comes to him. He does not believe. If he did, he would listen; but in religion he talks. If he did, he would accept a gift; but in religion he takes something for himself. If he did, he would let God himself intercede for God: but in religion he ventures to grasp at God. Because it is a grasping, religion is the contradiction of revelation, the concentrated expression of human unbelief, i.e. an attitude and activity which is directly opposed to faith. It is a feeble but defiant, an arrogant but hopeless, attempt to create something which man could do, but now cannot do, or can do only because and if God himself creates it for him: the knowledge of the truth, the knowledge of God. We cannot therefore interpret the attempt as a harmonious co-operating of man with the revelation of God, as though religion were a kind of outstretched hand which is filled by God in his revelation. Again, we cannot say of the evident religious capacity of man that it is, so to speak, the general form of human knowledge, which acquires its true and proper content in the shape of revelation. On the contrary, we have here an exclusive contradiction. In religion man bolts and bars himself against revelation by providing a substitute, by taking away in advance the very thing which has to be given by God . . .

He has, of course, the power to do this. But what he achieves and acquires in virtue of this power is never the knowledge of God as Lord and God. It is never the truth.

It is a complete fiction, which has not only little but no relation to God. It is an anti-God who has first to be known as such and discarded when the truth comes to him. But it can be known as such, as a fiction, only as the truth does come to him . . .

Revelation does not link up with a human religion which is already present and practised. It contradicts it, just as religion previously contradicted revelation. It displaces it, just as religion previously displaced revelation; just as faith cannot link up with a mistaken faith, but must contradict and displace it as unbelief, as an act of contradiction . . .

2. As the self-offering and self-manifestation of God, revelation is the act by which in grace he reconciles man to himself by grace. As a radical teaching about God, it is also the radical assistance of God which comes to us as those who are unrighteous and unholy, and as such damned and lost. In this respect, too, the affirmation which revelation makes and presupposes of man is that he is unable to help himself either in whole or even in part. But again, he ought not to have been so helpless. It is not inherent in the nature and concept of man that he should be unrighteous and unholy and therefore damned and lost. He was created to be the image of God, i.e. to obedience towards God and not to sin, to salvation and not to destruction. But he is not summoned to this as to a state in which he might still somehow find himself, but as one in which he no longer finds himself, from which he has fallen by his own fault. But this, too, is a truth which he cannot maintain: it is not present to him unless it comes to him in revelation, i.e. in Jesus Christ, to be declared to him in a new way – the oldest truth of all in a way which is quite new. He cannot in any sense declare to himself that he is righteous and holy, and therefore saved, for in his own mouth as his own judgement of himself it would

be a lie. It is truth as the revealed knowledge of God. It is truth in Jesus Christ. Jesus Christ does not fill out and improve all the different attempts of man to think of God and to represent him according to his own standard. But as the self-offering and self-manifestation of God he replaces and completely outbids those attempts, putting them in the shadows to which they belong. Similarly, in so far as God reconciles the world to himself in him, he replaces all the different attempts of man to reconcile God to the world, all our human efforts at justification and sanctification, at conversion and salvation. The revelation of God in Jesus Christ maintains that our justification and sanctification, our conversion and salvation, have been brought about and achieved once and for all in Jesus Christ. And our faith in Jesus Christ consists in our recognizing and admitting and affirming and accepting the fact that everything has actually been done for us once and for all in Jesus Christ. He is the assistance that comes to us. He alone is the Word of God that is spoken to us. There is an exchange of status between him and us: his righteousness and holiness are ours, our sin is his; he is lost for us, and we for his sake are saved. By this exchange (καταλλαγή, 2 Corinthians 5:19) revelation stands or falls. It would not be the active, redemptive self-offering and self-manifestation of God, if it were not centrally and decisively the *satisfactio* and *intercessio Jesu Christi*.

And now we can see a second way in which revelation contradicts religion, and conversely religion necessarily opposes revelation. For what is the purpose of the universal attempt of religions to anticipate God, to foist a human product into the place of his Word, to make our own images of the one who is known only where he gives himself to be known, images which are first spiritual, and then religious, and then actually visible? What does the religious man want when he thinks and believes and maintains that there is a unique and ultimate and decisive being, that there is a divine being (θεῖον), a godhead, that there are gods and a single supreme God, and when he thinks that he himself is posited, determined, conditioned, and overruled by this being? Is the postulate of God or gods, and the need to objectify the Ultimate spiritually or physically, conditioned by man's experience of the actual superiority and lordship of certain natural and supernatural, historical and eternal necessities, potencies, and ordinances? Is this experience (or the postulate and need which correspond to it) followed by the feeling of man's impotence and failure in face of this higher world, by the urge to put himself on peaceful and friendly terms with it, to interest it on his behalf, to assure himself of its support, or better still, to enable himself to exercise an influence on it, to participate in its power and dignity and to co-operate in its work? Does man's attempt to justify and sanctify himself follow the attempt to think of God and represent him? Or is the relationship the direct opposite? Is the primary thing man's obscure urge to justify and sanctify himself, i.e. to confirm and strengthen himself in the awareness and exercise of his skill and strength to master life, to come to terms with the world, to make the world serviceable to him? Is religion with its dogmatics and worship and precepts the most primitive, or better perhaps, the most intimate and intensive part of the technique, by which we try to come to terms with life? Is it that the experience of that higher world, or the need to objectify it in the thought of God and the representation of God, must be regarded only as an exponent of this attempt, that is, as the ideal construction inevitable within the framework of this technique? Are the gods only reflected images and guarantees of the needs and capacities of man, who in reality is lonely and driven back upon himself and his own willing and ordering and creating? Are sacrifice and prayer and asceticism and morality more basic than God and the gods? Who is to say? In face of the two possibilities we are in a circle which we can consider from any point of view with exactly the same result. What is certain is that in respect of the practical content of religion it is still a matter of an attitude and activity which does not correspond to God's revelation, but contradicts it. At this point, too, weakness and defiance, helplessness and arrogance, folly and imagination are so close to one another that we can scarcely distinguish the one from the other. Where we want what is wanted in religion, i.e. justification and sanctification as our own work, we do not find ourselves – and it does not matter whether the thought and representation of God has a primary or only a secondary importance – on the direct way to God, who can then bring us to our goal at some higher stage on the way. On the contrary, we lock the door against God, we alienate ourselves from him, we come into direct opposition to him. God in his revelation will not allow man to try to come to terms with life, to justify and sanctify himself. God in his revelation, God in Jesus Christ, is the one who takes on himself the sin of the world, who wills that all our care should be cast upon him, because he careth for us . . .

It is the characteristically pious element in the pious effort to reconcile him to us which must be an abomination to God, whether idolatry is regarded as its presupposition or its result, or perhaps as both. Not by any continuing along this way, but only by radically breaking away from it, can we come, not to our own goal but to God's goal, which is the direct opposite of our goal . . .

TRUE RELIGION

The preceding expositions have established the fact that we can speak of 'true religion' only in the sense in which we speak of a 'justified sinner'.

Religion is never true in itself and as such. The revelation of God denies that any religion is true, i.e. that it is in truth the knowledge and worship of God and the reconciliation of man with God. For as the self-offering and self-manifestation of God, as the work of peace which God himself has concluded between himself and man, revelation is the truth beside which there is no other truth, over against which there is only lying and wrong. If by the concept of a 'true religion' we mean truth which belongs to religion in itself and as such, it is just as unattainable as a 'good man', if by goodness we mean something which man can achieve on his own initiative. No religion is true. It can only become true, i.e. according to that which it purports to be and for which it is upheld. And it can become true only in the way in which man is justified, from without; i.e. not of its own nature and being but only in virtue of a reckoning and adopting and separating which are foreign to its own nature and being, which are quite inconceivable from its own standpoint, which come to it quite apart from any qualifications or merits. Like justified man, true religion is a creature of grace. But grace is the revelation of God. No religion can stand before it as true religion. No man is righteous in its presence. It subjects us all to the judgement of death. But it can also call dead men to life and sinners to repentance. And similarly in the wider sphere where it shows all religion to be false, it can also create true religion. The abolishing of religion by revelation need not mean only its negation: the judgement that religion is unbelief. Religion can just as well be exalted in revelation, even though the judgement still stands. It can be upheld by it and concealed in it. It can be justified by it, and – we must at once add – sanctified. Revelation can adopt religion and mark it off as true religion. And it not only can. How do we come to assert that it can, if it has not already done so? There is a true religion: just as there are justified sinners. If we abide strictly by that analogy – and we are dealing not merely with an analogy, but in a comprehensive sense with the thing itself – we need have no hesitation in saying that the Christian religion is the true religion.

In our discussion of 'religion as unbelief' we did not consider the distinction between Christian and non-Christian religion. Our intention was that whatever we said about the other religions affected the Christian similarly. In the framework of that discussion we could not speak in any special way about Christianity. We could not give it any special or assured place in face of that judgement. Therefore the discussion cannot be understood as a preliminary polemic against the non-Christian religions, with a view to the ultimate assertion that the Christian religion is the true religion. If this were the case our task now would be to prove that, as distinct from the non-Christian religions, the Christian is not guilty of idolatry and self-righteousness, that it is not therefore unbelief but faith, and therefore true religion; or, which comes to the same thing, that it is no religion at all, but as against all religions, including their mystical and atheistical self-criticism, it is in itself the true and holy and as such the unspotted and incontestable form of fellowship between God and man. To enter on this path would be to deny the very thing we have to affirm. If the statement is to have any content we can dare to state that the Christian religion is the true one only as we listen to the divine revelation. But a statement which we dare to make as we listen to the divine revelation can only be a statement of faith. And a statement of faith is necessarily a statement which is thought and expressed in faith and from faith, i.e. in recognition and respect of what we are told by revelation. Its explicit and implicit content is unreservedly conditioned by what we are told. But that is certainly not the case if we try to reach the statement that the Christian religion is the true religion by a road which begins by leaving behind the judgement of revelation, that religion is unbelief, as a matter which does not apply to us Christians but only to others, the non-Christians, thus enabling us to separate and differentiate ourselves from them with the help of this judgement. On the contrary, it is our business as Christians to apply this judgement first and most acutely to ourselves: and to others, the non-Christians, only in so far as we recognize ourselves in them, i.e. only as we see in them the truth of this judgement of revelation which concerns us, in the solidarity, therefore, in which, anticipating them in both repentance and hope, we accept this judgement to participate in the promise of revelation. At the end of the road we have to tread there is, of course, the promise to those who accept God's judgement, who let themselves be led beyond their unbelief. There is faith in this promise, and, in this faith, the presence and reality of the grace of God, which, of course, differentiates our religion, the Christian, from all others as the true religion. This exalted goal cannot be reached except by this humble road. And it would not be a truly humble road if we tried to tread it except in the consciousness that any 'attaining' here can consist only in the utterly humble and thankful adoption of something which we would not attain if it were not already attained in God's revelation before we set out on the road.

We must insist, therefore, that at the beginning of a knowledge of truth of the Christian religion there stands the recognition that this religion, too, stands under the judgement that religion is unbelief, and that it is not acquitted by any inward worthiness, but only by the grace of God, proclaimed and effectual in his revelation. But concretely this judgement affects the whole practice of our faith: our Christian conceptions of God and the things of God, our Christian theology, our Christian worship, our forms of Christian fellowship and order, our Christian morals, poetry, and art, our attempts to give individual and social form to the Christian life, our Christian strategy and tactics in the interest of our Christian cause, in short our Christianity, to the extent that it is *our* Christianity, the human work which we undertake and adjust to all kinds of near and remote aims and which as such is seen to be on the same level as the human work in other religions. This judgement means that all this Christianity of ours, and all the details of it, are not as such what they ought to be and pretend to be, a work of faith, and therefore of obedience to the divine revelation. What we have here is in its own way – a different way from that of other religions, but no less seriously – unbelief, i.e. opposition to the divine revelation, and therefore active idolatry and self-righteousness. It is the same helplessness and arbitrariness. It is the same self-exaltation of man which means his most profound abasement. But this time it is in place of and in opposition to the self-manifestation and self-offering of God, the reconciliation which God himself has accomplished, it is in disregard of the divine consolations and admonitions that great and small Babylonian towers are erected, which cannot as such be pleasing to God, since they are definitely not set up to his glory . . .

We are here concerned with an order which can be forgotten or infringed only to the detriment of a real knowledge of the truth of the Christian religion. Again, to ascribe the demonstrative power for this truth to the religious self-consciousness as such is to the dishonouring of God and the eternal destruction of souls. Even outwardly, in its debate with non-Christian religions, the Church can never do more harm than when it thinks that it must abandon the apostolic injunction, that grace is sufficient for us. The place to which we prefer to look is only mist, and the reed upon which we have to lean will slip through our fingers. By trying to resist and conquer other religions, we put ourselves on the same level. They, too, appeal to this or that immanent truth in them. They, too, can triumph in the power of the religious self-consciousness, and sometimes they have been astonishingly successful over wide areas. Christianity can take part in this fight. There is no doubt that it does not lack the necessary equipment, and can give a good account of itself alongside the other religions. But do not forget that if it does this it has renounced its birthright. It has renounced the unique power which it has as the religion of revelation. This power dwells only in weakness. And it does not really operate, nor does the power with which Christianity hopes to work, the power of religious self-consciousness which is the gift of grace in the midst of weakness, unless Christianity has first humbled instead of exalting itself. By its neglect of this order, Christianity has created great difficulties for itself in its debate with other religions . . .

We must not allow ourselves to be confused by the fact that a history of Christianity can be written only as a story of the distress which it makes for itself. It is a story which lies completely behind the story of that which took place between Yahweh and his people, between Jesus and his apostles. It is a story whose source and meaning and goal, the fact that the Christian is strong only in his weakness, that he is really satisfied by grace, can in the strict sense nowhere be perceived directly. Not even in the history of the Reformation! What can be perceived in history is the attempt which the Christian makes, in continually changing forms, to consider and vindicate his religion as a work which is in itself upright and holy. But he continually feels himself thwarted and hampered and restrained by Holy Scripture, which does not allow this, which even seems to want to criticize this Christian religion of his. He obviously cannot shut out the recollection that it is in respect of this very work of his religion that he cannot dispense with the grace of God and therefore stands under the judgement of God. At this point we are particularly reminded of the history of the Reformation. But in the very light of that history we see that the recollection has always been there, even in the pre- and post-Reformation periods. Yet the history of Christianity as a whole reveals a tendency which is quite contrary to this recollection. It would be arbitrary not to recognize this, and to claim that the history of Christianity, as distinct from that of other religions, is the story of that part of humanity, which, as distinct from others, has existed only as the part which of grace lives by grace. In the strict sense there is no evidence of this throughout the whole range of Christianity. What is evident is in the first instance a part of humanity which no less contradicts the grace and revelation of God because it claims them as its own peculiar and most sacred treasures, and its religion is to that extent a religion of revelation. Contradiction is contradiction. That it exists at this point, in respect of the religion of revelation, can be denied even less than at other points. Elsewhere we might claim an extenuation that it simply exists in fact, but not in direct contrast with revelation. But in the history of Christianity, just because it is the religion of revelation, the sin is, as it were, committed with a high hand. Yes, sin! For contradiction against grace is unbelief, and unbelief is sin, indeed it is *the* sin. It is therefore a fact that we can speak of the truth of the Christian religion only within the doctrine of the *iustificatio impii.* The statement that even Christianity is unbelief gives rise to a whole mass of naïve and rationalizing contradictions. Church history itself is a history of this contradiction. But it is this very fact which best shows us how true and right the statement is. We can as little avoid the contradiction as jump over our own shadow.

We cannot expect that at a fourth or fifth or sixth stage the history of Christianity will be anything but a history of the distress which Christianity creates for itself. May it not lack in future reformation, i.e. expressions of warning and promise deriving from Holy Scripture! But before the end of all things we cannot expect that the Christian will not always show himself an enemy of grace, in spite of all intervening restraints.

Notwithstanding the contradiction and therefore our own existence, we can and must perceive that for our part we and our contradiction against grace stand under the even more powerful contradiction of grace itself. We can and must – in faith. To believe means, in the knowledge of our sin to rely upon the righteousness of God which makes an infinite satisfaction for our sin. Concretely, it means, in the knowledge of our contradiction against grace to cleave to the grace of God which infinitely contradicts this contradiction. In this knowledge of grace, in the knowledge that it is the justification of the ungodly, that it is grace for the enemies of grace, the Christian faith attains to its knowledge of the truth of the Christian religion. There can be no more question of any immanent rightness or holiness of this particular religion as the ground and content of the truth of it than there can be of any other religion claiming to be the true religion in virtue of its inherent advantages. The Christian cannot avoid abandoning any such claim. He cannot avoid confessing that he is a sinner even in his best actions as a Christian. And that is not, of course, the ground, but the symptom of the truth of the Christian religion. The abandoning and confessing means that the Christian Church is the place where, confronted with the revelation and grace of God, by grace men live by grace...

There is, of course, one fact which powerfully and decisively confirms the assertion, depriving it of its arbitrary character and giving to it a necessity which is absolute. But to discern this fact, our first task – and again and again we shall have to return to this 'first' – must be to ignore the whole realm of 'facts' which we and other human observers as such can discern and assess. For the fact about which we are speaking stands in the same relationship to this realm as does the sun to the earth. That the sun lights up this part of the earth and not that means for the earth no less than this, that day rules in the one part and night in the other. Yet the earth is the same in both places. In neither place is there anything in the earth itself to dispose it for the day. Apart from the sun, it would everywhere be enwrapped in eternal night. The fact that it is partly in the day does not derive in any sense from the nature of the particular part as such. Now it is in exactly the same way that the light of the righteousness and judgement of God falls upon the world of man's religion, upon one part of that world, upon the Christian religion, so that that religion is not in the night but in the day, it is not perverted but straight, it is not false religion but true. Taken by itself, it is still human religion and therefore unbelief, like all other religions. Neither in the root nor in the crown of this particular tree, neither at the source nor at the outflow of this particular stream, neither on the surface nor in the depth of this particular part of humanity can we point to anything that makes it suitable for the day of divine righteousness and judgement. If the Christian religion is the right and true religion the reason for it does not reside in facts which might point to itself or its own adherents, but in the fact which as the righteousness and the judgement of God confronts it as it does all other religions, characterizing and differentiating it and not one of the others as the right and true religion . . .

3. CHRISTIANITY AND THE NON-CHRISTIAN RELIGIONS

Karl Rahner

The following expositions are the notes of a lecture given on 28 April 1961 in Eichstätt (Bavaria) at a meeting of the Abendländische Akademie. *No attempt has been made to enlarge these notes here, although a great deal in them remains extremely fragmentary.*

'Open Catholicism' involves two things. It signifies the fact that the Catholic Church is opposed by historical forces which she herself cannot disregard as if they were purely 'worldly' forces and a matter of indifference to her but which, on the contrary, although they do not stand in a positive relationship of peace and mutual recognition to the Church, do have a significance for her. 'Open Catholicism' means also the task of becoming related to these forces in order to understand their existence (since this cannot be simply acknowledged), in order to bear with and overcome the annoyance of their opposition and in order to form the Church in such a way that she will be able to overcome as much of this pluralism as should not exist, by understanding herself as the higher unity of this opposition. 'Open Catholicism' means therefore a certain attitude towards the present-day pluralism of powers with different outlooks on the world. We do not, of course, refer to pluralism merely as a fact which one simply acknowledges without explaining it. Pluralism is meant here as a fact which ought to be thought about and one which, without denying that – in part at least – it should not exist at all, should be incorporated once more from a more elevated viewpoint into the totality and unity of the Christian understanding of human existence. For Christianity, one of the gravest elements of this pluralism in which we live and with which we must come to terms, and indeed the element most difficult to incorporate, is the pluralism of religions. We do not refer by this to the pluralism of Christian denominations. This pluralism too is a fact, and a challenge and task for Christians. But we are not concerned with it here.

Our subject is the more serious problem, at least in its ultimate and basic form, of the different religions which still exist even in Christian times, and this after a history and mission of Christianity which has already lasted two thousand years. It is true, certainly, that all these religions together, including Christianity, are faced today with an enemy which did not exist for them in the past. We refer to the decided lack of religion and the denial of religion in general. This denial, in a sense, takes the stage with the ardour of a religion and of an absolute and sacred system which is the basis and the yard-stick of all further thought. This denial, organized on the basis of a State, represents itself as *the* religion of the future – as the decided, absolute secularization of human existence excluding all mystery. No matter how paradoxical this may sound, it does remain true that precisely this state of siege in which religion in general finds itself, finds one of its most important weapons and opportunities for success in the fact that humanity is so torn in its religious adherence. But quite apart from this, this pluralism is a greater threat and a reason for greater unrest for Christianity than for any other religion. For no other religion – not even Islam – maintains so absolutely that it is *the* religion, the one and only valid revelation of the one living God, as does the Christian religion.

The fact of the pluralism of religions, which endures and still from time to time becomes virulent anew even after a history of two thousand years, must therefore be the greatest scandal and the greatest vexation for Christianity. And the threat of this vexation is also greater for the individual Christian today than ever before. For in the past, the other religion was in practice the religion of a completely different cultural environment. It belonged to a history with which the individual only communicated very much on the periphery of his own history; it was the religion of those who were even in every other respect alien to oneself. It is not surprising, therefore, that people did not wonder at the fact that these 'others' and 'strangers' had also a different religion. No wonder that in general people could not seriously consider these other religions as a challenge posed to themselves or even as a possibility for themselves. Today things have changed. The West is no longer shut up in itself; it can no longer regard itself simply as the centre of the history of this world and as the centre of culture, with a religion which even from this point of view (i.e. from a point of view which has really nothing to do with a decision of faith but which simply carries the weight of something quite self-evident) could appear as the obvious and indeed sole way of honouring God to be thought of for a European. Today everybody is the next-door neighbour and spiritual neighbour of everyone else in the world. And so everybody today is determined by the inter-communication of all those situations of life which affect the whole world. Every religion which exists in the world is – just like all cultural possibilities and actualities of other people – a question posed, and a possibility offered, to every person. And just as one experiences someone else's culture in practice as something relative to one's own and as something existentially demanding, so it is also involuntarily with alien religions. They have become part of one's own existential situation – no longer merely theoretically but in the concrete – and we experience them therefore as something which puts the absolute claim of our own Christian faith into question. Hence, the question about the understanding of and the continuing existence of religious pluralism as a factor of our immediate Christian existence is an urgent one and part of the question as to how we are to deal with today's pluralism.

This problem could be tackled from different angles. In the present context we simply wish to try to describe a few of those basic traits of a Catholic dogmatic interpretation of the non-Christian religions which may help us to come closer to a solution of the question about the Christian position in regard to the religious pluralism in the world of today. Since it cannot be said, unfortunately, that Catholic theology – as practised in more recent times – has really paid sufficient attention to the questions to be posed here, it will also be impossible to maintain that what we will have to say here can be taken as the common thought of Catholic theology. What we have to say carries, therefore, only as much weight as the reasons we can adduce, which reasons can again only be briefly indicated. Whenever the propositions to be mentioned carry a greater weight than this in theology, anyone trained in theology will realize it quite clearly from what is said. When we say that it is a question here of a *Catholic* dogmatic interpretation of the non-Christian religions, this is not meant to indicate that it is necessarily a question also of theories controverted among Christians themselves. It simply means that we will not be able to enter explicitly into the question as to whether the theses to be stated here can also hope to prove acceptable to Protestant theology. We say too that we are going to give a dogmatic interpretation, since we will pose our question not as empirical historians of religion but out of the self-understanding of Christianity itself, i.e. as dogmatic theologians.

1st Thesis: We must begin with the thesis which follows, because it certainly represents the basis in the Christian faith of the theological understanding of other religions. This thesis states that Christianity understands itself as the absolute religion, intended for all men, which cannot recognize any other religion beside itself as of equal right. This proposition is self-evident and basic for Christianity's understanding of itself. There is no need here to prove it or to develop its meaning. After all, Christianity does not take valid and lawful religion to mean primarily that relationship of man to God which man himself institutes on his own authority. Valid and lawful religion does not mean man's own interpretation of human existence. It is not the reflection and objectification of the experience which man has of himself and by himself.

Valid and lawful religion for Christianity is rather God's action on men, God's free self-revelation by communicating himself to man. It is God's relationship to men, freely instituted by God himself and revealed by God in this institution. *This* relationship of God to man is basically the same for all men, because it rests on the Incarnation, death and resurrection of the one Word of God become flesh. Christianity is God's own interpretation in his Word of this relationship of God to man founded in Christ by God himself. And so Christianity can recognize itself as the true and lawful religion for all men only where and when it enters with existential power and demanding force into the realm of another religion and – judging it by itself

– puts it in question. Since the time of Christ's coming – ever since he came in the flesh as the Word of God in absoluteness and reconciled, i.e. united the world with God by his death and resurrection, not merely theoretically but really – Christ and his continuing historical presence in the world (which we call 'Church') is *the* religion which binds man to God.

Already we must, however, make one point clear as regards this first thesis (which cannot be further developed and proved here). It is true that the Christian religion itself has its own pre-history which traces this religion back to the beginning of the history of humanity – even though it does this by many basic steps. It is also true that this fact of having a pre-history is of much greater importance, according to the evidence of the New Testament, for the theoretical and practical proof of the claim to absolute truth made by the Christian religion than our current fundamental theology is aware of. Nevertheless, the Christian religion as such has a beginning in history; it did not always exist but began at some point in time. It has not always and everywhere been *the* way of salvation for men – at least not in its historically tangible ecclesio-sociological constitution and in the reflex fruition of God's saving activity in, and in view of, Christ. As a historical quantity Christianity has, therefore, a temporal and spatial starting point in Jesus of Nazareth and in the saving event of the unique Cross and the empty tomb in Jerusalem. It follows from this, however, that this absolute religion – even when it begins to be this for practically all men – must come in a historical way to men, facing them as the only legitimate and demanding religion for them. It is therefore a question of whether this moment, when the existentially real demand is made by the absolute religion in its historically tangible form, takes place really at the same chronological moment for all people, or whether the occurrence of this moment has itself a history and thus is not chronologically simultaneous for all people, cultures and spaces of history. (This is a question which up until now Catholic theology has not thought through with sufficient clarity and reflection by really confronting it with the length and intricacy of real human time and history.) Normally the beginning of the objective obligation of the Christian message for all men – in other words, the abolition of the validity of the Mosaic religion *and* of all other religions which (as we will see later) may also have a period of validity and of being-willed-by-God – is thought to occur in the apostolic age. Normally, therefore, one regards the time between this beginning and the actual acceptance of the personally guilty refusal of Christianity in a non-Jewish world and history as the span between the already given promulgation of the law and the moment when the one to whom the law refers takes cognizance of it.

It is not just an idle academic question to ask whether such a conception is correct or whether, as we maintain, there could be a different opinion in this matter, i.e. whether one could hold that the beginning of Christianity for actual periods of history, for cultures and religions, could be postponed to those moments in time when Christianity became a real historical factor in an individual history and culture – a real historical moment in a particular culture. For instance, one concludes from the first, usual answer that *everywhere* in the world, since the first Pentecost, baptism of children dying before reaching the use of reason is necessary for their supernatural salvation, although this was not necessary before that time. For other questions, too, a correct and considered solution of the present question could be of great importance, as for instance for the avoidance of immature conversions, for the justification and importance of 'indirect' missionary work, etc. One will have to ask oneself whether one can still agree today with the first opinion mentioned above, in view of the history of the missions which has already lasted two thousand years and yet is still to a great extent in its beginnings – for even Suarez himself, for instance, had already seen (at least with regard to the *Jews*) that the *promulgatio* and *obligatio* of the Christian religion, and not merely the *divulgatio* and *notitia promulgationis*, take place in historical sequence. We cannot really answer this question here, but it may at least be pointed out as an open question; in practice, the correctness of the second theory may be presupposed since it alone corresponds to the real historicity of Christianity and salvation-history.

From this there follows a delicately differentiated understanding of our first thesis: we maintain positively only that, as regards destination, Christianity is the absolute and hence the only religion for all men. We leave it, however, an open question (at least in principle) at what exact point in time the absolute obligation of the Christian religion has in fact come into effect for every man and culture, even in the sense of the *objective* obligation of such a demand. Nevertheless – and this leaves the thesis formulated still sufficiently exciting – wherever in practice Christianity reaches man in the real urgency and rigour of his actual existence, Christianity – once understood – presents itself as the only still valid religion for this man, a necessary means for his salvation and not merely an obligation with the necessity of a precept. It should be noted that this is a question of the necessity of a *social* form for salvation. Even though this is Christianity and not some other religion, it may surely still be said without hesitation that this thesis contains implicitly another thesis which states that in concrete human existence as such, the nature of religion itself must include a social constitution – which means that religion can exist only in a social form. This means, therefore, that man, who is commanded to have a religion, is also commanded to seek and accept a social form of religion. It will soon become clear what this reflection implies for the estimation of non-Christian religions.

Finally, we may mention one further point in this connection. What is vital in the *notion* of *paganism* and hence also of the non-Christian pagan religions (taking 'pagan' here as a theological concept without any disparaging intent) is not the actual refusal to accept the Christian religion but the absence of any sufficient historical encounter with Christianity which would have enough historical power to render the Christian religion really present in this pagan society and in the history of the people concerned. If this is so, then paganism ceases to exist in this sense by reason of what is happening today. For the Western world is opening out into a universal world history in which every people and every cultural sector becomes an inner factor of every other people and every other cultural sector. Or rather, paganism is slowly entering a new phase: there is *one* history of the world, and in this *one* history both the Christians and the non-Christians (i.e. the old and new pagans together) live in one and the same situation and face each other in dialogue; and thus the question of the theological meaning of the other religions arises once more and with even greater urgency.

2nd Thesis: Until the moment when the Gospel really enters into the historical situation of an individual, a non-Christian religion (even outside the Mosaic religion) does not merely contain elements of a natural knowledge of

God, elements, moreover, mixed up with human depravity which is the result of original sin and later aberrations. It contains also supernatural elements arising out of the grace which is given to men as a gratuitous gift on account of Christ. For this reason a non-Christian religion can be recognized as a *lawful* religion (although only in different degrees) without thereby denying the error and depravity contained in it. This thesis requires a more extensive explanation.

We must first of all note the point up to which this evaluation of the non-Christian religions is valid. This is the point in time when the Christian religion becomes a historically real factor for those who are of this religion. Whether this point is the same, theologically speaking, as the first Pentecost, or whether it is different in chronological time for individual peoples and religions, is something which even at this point will have to be left to a certain extent an open question. We have, however, chosen our formulation in such a way that it points more in the direction of the opinion which seems to us the more correct one in the matter although the *criteria* for a more exact determination of this moment in time must again be left an open question.

The thesis itself is divided into two parts. It means first of all that it is *a priori* quite possible to suppose that there are supernatural, grace-filled elements in non-Christian religions. Let us first of all deal with this statement. It does not mean, of course, that all the elements of a polytheistic conception of the divine, and all the other religious, ethical and metaphysical aberrations contained in the non-Christian religions, are to be or may be treated as harmless either in theory or in practice. There have been constant protests against such elements throughout the history of Christianity and throughout the history of the

Christian interpretation of the non-Christian religions, starting with the Epistle to the Romans and following on the Old Testament polemics against the religion of the 'heathens'. Every one of these protests is still valid in what was really meant and expressed by them. Every such protest remains a part of the message which Christianity and the Church has to give to the peoples who profess such religions. Furthermore, we are not concerned here with an *a posteriori* history of religions. Consequently, we also cannot describe empirically what should not exist and what is opposed to God's will in these non-Christian religions, nor can we represent these things in their many forms and degrees. We are here concerned with dogmatic theology and so can merely repeat the universal and unqualified verdict as to the unlawfulness of the non-Christian religions right from the moment when they came into real and historically powerful contact with Christianity (and at first only thus!). It is clear, however, that this condemnation does not mean to deny the very basic differences within the non-Christian religions especially since the pious, God-pleasing pagan was already a theme of the Old Testament, and especially since this God-pleasing pagan cannot simply be thought of as living absolutely outside the concrete socially constituted religion and constructing his own religion on his native foundations – just as St Paul in his speech on the Areopagus did not simply exclude a positive and basic view of the pagan religion.

The decisive reason for the first part of our thesis is basically a theological consideration. This consideration (prescinding from certain more precise qualifications) rests ultimately on the fact that, if we wish to be Christians, we must profess belief in the universal and serious salvific purpose of God towards all men which is true even within the post-paradisean phase of salvation dominated by original sin. We know, to be sure, that this proposition of faith does not say anything certain about the *individual* salvation of man understood as something which has in fact been reached. But God desires the salvation of everyone. And this salvation willed by God is the salvation won by Christ, the salvation of supernatural grace which divinizes man, the salvation of the beatific vision. It is a salvation really intended for all those millions upon millions of people who lived perhaps a million years before Christ – and also for those who have lived after Christ – in nations, cultures and epochs of a very wide range which were still completely shut off from the viewpoint of those living in the light of the New Testament. If, on the one hand, we conceive salvation as something specifically *Christian*, if there is no salvation apart from Christ, if according to Catholic teaching the supernatural divinization of mankind can never be replaced merely by good-will on the part of man but is necessary as something itself given in this earthly life; and if, on the other hand, God has really, truly and seriously intended this salvation for all men – then these two aspects cannot be reconciled in any other way than by stating that every human being is really and truly exposed to the influence of divine, supernatural grace which offers an interior union with God and by means of which God communicates himself whether the individual takes up an attitude of acceptance or of refusal towards this grace. It is senseless to suppose cruelly – and without any hope of acceptance by the man of today, in view of the enormous extent of the extra-Christian history of salvation and damnation – that nearly all men living outside the official and public Christianity are so evil and stubborn that the offer of supernatural grace ought not even to be made in fact in most cases, since these individuals have already rendered themselves unworthy of such an offer by previous, subjectively grave offences against the natural moral law.

If one gives more exact theological thought to this matter, then one cannot regard nature and grace as two phases in the life of the individual which follow each other in time. It is furthermore impossible to think that this offer of supernatural, divinizing grace made to all men on account of the universal salvific purpose of God, should in general (prescinding from the relatively few exceptions) remain ineffective in most cases on account of the personal guilt of the individual. For, as far as the Gospel is concerned, we have no really conclusive reason for thinking so pessimistically of men. On the other hand, and contrary to every merely human experience, we do have every reason for thinking optimistically of God and his salvific will which is more powerful than the extremely limited stupidity and evil-mindedness of men. However little we can say with certitude about the final lot of an individual inside or outside the officially constituted Christian religion, we have every reason to think optimistically – i.e. truly hopefully and confidently in a Christian sense – of God who has certainly the last word and who has revealed to us that he has spoken his powerful word of reconciliation and forgiveness into the world. If it is true that the eternal Word of God has become flesh and has died the death of sin for the sake of our salvation and in spite of our guilt, then the Christian has no right to suppose that the fate of the world – having regard to the whole of the world – takes the same course on account of man's refusal as it would have taken if Christ had not come. Christ and his salvation are not simply one of two possibilities offering themselves to man's free choice; they are the need of God which bursts open and redeems the false choice of man by overtaking it. In Christ God not only gives the *possibility* of salvation, which in that case would still have to be effected by man himself, but the actual salvation itself, however much this includes also the right decision of human freedom which is itself a gift from God. Where sin already existed, grace came in superabundance. And hence we have every right to suppose that grace has not only been offered even outside the Christian Church (to deny this would be the error of Jansenism) but also that, in a great many cases at least, grace gains the victory in man's free acceptance of it, this being again the result of grace.

Of course, we would have to show more explicitly than the shortness of time permits that the empirical picture of human beings, their life, their religion and their individual and universal history does not disprove this optimism of a faith which knows the whole world to be subjected to the salvation won by Christ. But we must remember that the theoretical and ritualistic factors in good and evil are only a very inadequate expression of what man actually accomplishes in practice. We must remember that the same transcendence of man (even the transcendence elevated and liberated by God's grace) can be exercised in many different ways and under the most varied labels. We must take into consideration that whenever the religious person acts really religiously, he makes use of, or omits unthinkingly, the manifold forms of religious institutions by making a consciously critical choice among and between them. We must consider the immeasurable difference – which it seems right to suppose to exist even in the Christian sphere – between what is objectively wrong in moral life and the extent to which this is really realized with subjectively grave guilt. Once we take all this into consideration, we will not hold it to be impossible that grace is at work, and is even being accepted, in the spiritual, personal life of the individual, no matter how primitive, unenlightened, apathetic and earth-bound such a life may at first sight appear to be. We can say quite simply that, wherever, and in so far as, the individual makes a moral decision in his life (and where could this be declared to be in any way absolutely impossible – except in precisely 'pathological' cases?), this moral decision can also be thought to measure up to the character of a supernaturally elevated, believing and thus saving act, and hence to be more in actual fact than merely 'natural morality'. Hence, if one believes seriously in the universal salvific purpose of God towards all men in Christ, it need not and cannot really be doubted that gratuitous influences of properly Christian supernatural grace are conceivable in the life of all men (provided they are first of all regarded as individuals) and that these influences can be presumed to be accepted in spite of the sinful state of men and in spite of their apparent estrangement from God.

Our second thesis goes even further than this, however, and states in its second part that, from what has been said, the actual religions of 'pre-Christian' humanity too must not be regarded as simply illegitimate from the very start, but must be seen as quite capable of having a positive significance. This statement must naturally be taken in a very different sense which we cannot examine here for the various particular religions. This means that the different religions will be able to lay claim to being lawful religions only in very different senses and to very different degrees. But precisely this variability is not at all excluded by the notion of a 'lawful religion', as we will have to show in a moment. A lawful religion means here an institutional religion whose 'use' by man at a certain period can be regarded on the whole as a positive means of gaining the right relationship to God and thus for the attaining of salvation, a means which is therefore positively included in God's plan of salvation.

That such a notion and the reality to which it refers can exist even where such a religion shows many theoretical and practical errors in its concrete form becomes clear in a theological analysis of the structure of the Old Covenant. We must first of all remember in this connection that only in the New Testament – in the Church of Christ understood as something which is eschatologically final and *hence* (and only for this reason) 'indefectible' and infallible – is there realized the notion of a Church which, because it is instituted by God in some way or other, already contains the permanent norm of differentiation between what is right (i.e. willed by God) and what is wrong in the religious sphere, and contains it both as a permanent institution and as an intrinsic element of this religion. There was nothing like this in the Old Testament, although it must undoubtedly be recognized as a lawful religion. The Old Covenant – understood as a concrete, historical and religious manifestation – contained what is right, willed by God, *and* what is false, erroneous, wrongly developed and depraved. But there was no permanent, continuing and institutional court of appeal in the Old Covenant which could have differentiated authoritatively, always and with certainty for the conscience of the individual between what was willed by God and what was due to human corruption in the actual religion. Of course, there were the prophets. They were not a permanent institution, however, but a conscience which had always to assert itself anew on behalf of the people in order to protest against the corruption of the religion as it existed at the time, thus – incidentally – confirming the existence of this corruption. The official, institutional forms known as the 'kingdom' and the priesthood were so little proof against this God-offending corruption that they could bring about the ruin of the Israelitic religion itself. And since there were also pseudo-prophets, and no infallible 'institutional' court of appeal for distinguishing genuine and false prophecy, it was – in the last analysis – left to the conscience of the individual Israelite himself to differentiate between what in the concrete appearance of the Israelitic religion was the true covenant with God and what was a humanly free, and so in certain cases falsifying, interpretation and corruption of this God-instituted religion. There might have been objective criteria for such a distinction of spirits, but their application could not simply be left to an 'ecclesiastical' court – not even in the most decisive questions – since official judgements could be wrong even about these questions and in fact were completely wrong about them.

This and nothing more – complete with its distinction between what was willed by God and what was human, all too human, a distinction which was ultimately left to be decided by the individual – was the concrete Israelitic religion. The Holy Scriptures do indeed give us the official and valid deposit to help us differentiate among the spirits which moved the history of the Old Testament religion. But since the infallible delimitation of the canon of the Old Testament is again to be found only in the New Testament, the exact and final differentiation between the lawful and the unlawful in the Old Testament religion is again possible only by making use of the New Testament as something eschatologically final. The unity of the concrete religion of the Old Testament, which (ultimately) could be distinguished only gropingly and at one's own risk, was however the unity willed by God, providential for the Israelites in the order of salvation and indeed the lawful religion for them. In this connection it must furthermore be taken into consideration that it was meant to be this only for the Israelites and for no one else; the institution of those belonging to the Jewish religion without being of the Jewish race (i.e. of the proselytes), was a very much later phenomenon. Hence it cannot be a part of the notion of a lawful religion in the above sense that it should be free from corruption, error and objective moral wrong in the concrete form of its appearance, or that it should contain a clear objective and permanent final court of appeal for the conscience of the individual to enable the individual to differentiate clearly and with certainty between the elements willed and instituted by God and those which are merely human and corrupt.

We must therefore rid ourselves of the prejudice that we can face a non-Christian religion with the dilemma that it must either come from God in everything it contains and thus correspond to God's will and positive providence, or be simply a purely human construction. If man is under God's grace even in these religions – and to deny this is certainly absolutely wrong – then the possession of this supernatural grace cannot but show itself, and cannot but become a formative factor of life in the concrete, even where (though not only where) this life turns the relationship to the absolute into an explicit theme, viz. in religion. It would perhaps be possible to say in theory that where a certain religion is not only accompanied in its concrete appearance by something false and humanly corrupted but also makes this an explicitly and consciously adopted element – an explicitly declared condition of its *nature* – this religion is wrong in its deepest and most specific being and hence can no longer be regarded as a lawful religion – not even in the widest sense of the word. This may be quite correct in theory. But we must surely go on to ask whether there is any religion apart from the Christian religion (meaning here even only the Catholic religion) with an authority which could elevate falsehood into one of its really essential parts and which could thus face man with an alternative of either accepting this falsehood as the most real and decisive factor of the religion or leaving this religion. Even if one could perhaps say something like this of Islam as such, it would have to be denied of the majority of religions. It would have to be asked in every case to what extent the followers of such religions would actually agree with such an interpretation of their particular religion. If one considers furthermore how easily a concrete, originally religious act can be always directed in its intention towards one and the same absolute, even when it manifests itself in the most varied forms, then it will not even be possible to say that theoretical polytheism, however deplorable and objectionable it may be objectively, must always and everywhere be an absolute obstacle to the performance in such a religion of genuinely religious acts directed to the one true God. This is particularly true since it cannot be proved that the practical religious life of the ancient Israelites, in so far as it manifested itself in popular theory, was always more than mere henotheism.

Furthermore, it must be borne in mind that the individual ought to and must have the possibility in his life of partaking in a genuine saving relationship to God, and this at all times and in all situations of the history of the human race. Otherwise there could be no question of a serious and also actually effective salvific design of God for all men, in all ages and places. In view of the social nature of man and the previously even more radical social solidarity of men, however, it is quite unthinkable that man, being what he is, could actually achieve this relationship to God – which he must have and which if he is to be saved, is and must be made possible for him by God – in an absolutely private interior reality and this outside of the actual religious bodies which offer themselves to him in the environment in which he lives. If man had to be and could always and everywhere be a *homo religiosus* in order to be able to save himself as such, then he was this *homo religiosus* in the concrete religion in which 'people' lived and had to live at that time. He could not escape this religion, however much he may have and did take up a critical and selective attitude towards this religion on individual matters, and however much he may have and did put different stresses in practice on certain things which were at variance with the official theory of this religion. If, however, man can always have a positive, saving relationship to God, and if he always had to have it, then he has always had it within *that* religion which in practice was at his disposal by being a factor in his sphere of existence. As already stated above, the inherence of the individual exercise of religion in a social religious order is one of the essential traits of true religion as it exists in practice. Hence, if one were to expect from someone who lives outside the Christian religion that he should have exercised his genuine, saving relationship to God absolutely outside the religion which society offered him, then such a conception would turn religion into something intangibly interior, into something which is always and everywhere performed only indirectly, a merely transcendental religion without anything which could become tangible in categories. Such a conception would annul the above-mentioned principle regarding the necessarily social nature of all religion in the concrete, so that even the Christian Church would then no longer have the necessary presupposition of general human and natural law as proof of her necessity. And since it does not at all belong to the notion of a lawful religion intended by God for man as something positively salvific that it should be pure and positively willed by God in all its elements, such a religion can be called an absolutely legitimate religion for the person concerned. That which God has intended as salvation for him reached him, in accordance with God's will and by his permission (no longer adequately separable in practice), in the *concrete* religion of his actual realm of existence and historical condition, but this fact did not deprive him of the right and the limited possibility to criticize and to heed impulses of religious reform which by God's providence kept on recurring within such a religion. For a still better and simpler understanding of this, one has only to think of the natural and socially constituted morality of a people and culture. Such a morality is never pure but is always also corrupted, as Jesus confirmed even in the case of the Old Testament. It can always be disputed and corrected, therefore, by the individual in accordance with his conscience. Yet, taken in its totality, it is *the* way in which the individual encounters the natural divine law according to God's will, and the way in which the natural law is given real, actual power in the life of the individual who cannot reconstruct these tablets of the divine law anew on his own responsibility and as a private metaphysician.

The morality of a people and of an age, taken in its totality, is therefore the legitimate and concrete form of the divine law (even though, of course, it can and may have to be corrected), so that it was not until the New Testament that the institution guaranteeing the purity of this form became (with the necessary reservations) an element of this form itself. Hence, if there existed a divine moral law and religion in the life of man *before* this moment, then its absolute purity (i.e. its constitution by divinely willed elements alone) must not be made the condition of the lawfulness of its existence. In fact, if every man who comes into the world is pursued by God's grace – and if one of the effects of this grace, even in its supernatural and salvifically elevating form, is to cause changes in consciousness (as is maintained by the better theory in Catholic theology) even though it cannot be simply *as* such a direct object of certain reflection – then it cannot be true that the actually existing religions do not bear any trace of the fact that all men are in some way affected by grace. These traces may be difficult to distinguish even to the enlightened eye of the Christian. But they must be there. And perhaps we may only have looked too superficially and with too little love at the non-Christian religions and so have not really seen them. In any case it is certainly not right to regard them as new conglomerates of natural theistic metaphysics and as a humanly incorrect interpretation and institutionalization of this 'natural religion'. The religions existing in the concrete must contain supernatural, gratuitous elements, and in using *these* elements the pre-Christian was able to attain God's grace: presumably, too, the pre-Christian exists even to this day, even though the possibility is gradually disappearing *today.* If we say that there were lawful religions in pre-Christian ages even outside the realm of the Old Testament, this does not mean that these religions were lawful in *all* their elements – to maintain this would be absurd. Nor does it mean that *every* religion was lawful; for in certain cases several forms, systems and institutions of a religious kind offered themselves within the historically concrete situation of the particular member of a certain people, culture, period of history, etc., so that the person concerned had to decide as to *which* of them was here and now, and on the whole, the more correct way (and hence for him *in concreto* the only correct way) of finding God.

This thesis is not meant to imply that the lawfulness of

the Old Testament religion was of exactly the same kind as that which we are prepared to grant in a certain measure to the extra-Christian religions. For in the Old Testament the prophets saw to it (even though not by way of a permanent institution) that there existed a possibility of distinguishing in public salvation-history between what was lawful and what was unlawful in the history of the religion of the Israelites. This cannot be held to be true to the same extent outside this history, although this again does not mean that outside the Old Testament there could be no question of any kind of divinely guided salvation-history in the realm of public history and institutions.

The main difference between such a salvation-history and that of the Old Testament will presumably lie in the fact that the historical, factual nature of the New Testament has *its* immediate pre-history in the *Old Testament* (which pre-history, in parenthesis, is insignificantly brief in comparison with the general salvation-history which counts perhaps a million years – for the former can be known with any certainty only from the time of Abraham or of Moses). Hence, the New Testament unveils *this* short span of salvation-history distinguishing its divinely willed elements and those which are contrary to God's will. It does this by a distinction which we cannot make in the same way in the history of any other religion. The second part of this second thesis, however, states two things positively. It states that even religions other than the Christian and the Old Testament religions contain quite certainly elements of a supernatural influence by grace which must make itself felt even in these objectifications. And it also states that by the fact that in practice man as he really is can live his proffered relationship to God only in society, man must have had the right and indeed the duty to live this his relationship to God within the religious and social realities offered to him in his particular historical situation.

3rd Thesis: If the second thesis is correct, then Christianity does not simply confront the member of an extra-Christian religion as a mere non-Christian but as someone who can and must already be regarded in this or that respect as an anonymous Christian. It would be wrong to regard the pagan as someone who has not yet been touched in any way by God's grace and truth. If, however, he has experienced the grace of God – if, in certain circumstances, he has already accepted this grace as the ultimate, unfathomable entelechy of his existence by accepting the immeasurableness of his dying existence as opening out into infinity – then he has already been given revelation in a true sense even before he has been affected by missionary preaching from without. For this grace, understood as the *a priori* horizon of all his spiritual acts, accompanies his consciousness subjectively, even though it is not known objectively. And the revelation which comes to him from without is not in such a case the proclamation of something as yet absolutely unknown, in the sense in which one tells a child here in Bavaria, for the first time in school, that there is a continent called Australia. Such a revelation is then the expression in objective concepts of something which this person has already attained or could already have attained in the depth of his rational existence. It is not possible here to prove more exactly that this *fides implicita* is something which dogmatically speaking can occur in a so-called pagan. We can do no more here than to state our thesis and to indicate the direction in which the proof of this thesis might be found. But if it is true that a person who becomes the object of the Church's missionary efforts is or may be already someone on the way towards his salvation, and someone who in certain circumstances finds it, without being reached by the proclamation of the Church's message – and if it is at the same time true that this salvation which reaches him in this way is Christ's salvation, since there is no other salvation – then it must be possible to be not only an anonymous theist but also an anonymous Christian. And then it is quite true that in the last analysis, the proclamation of the Gospel does not simply turn someone absolutely abandoned by God and Christ into a Christian, but turns an anonymous Christian into someone who now also knows about his Christian belief in the depths of his grace-endowed being by objective reflection and in the profession of faith which is given a social form in the Church.

It is not thereby denied, but on the contrary implied, that this explicit self-realization of his previously anonymous Christianity is itself part of the development of this Christianity itself – a higher stage of development of this Christianity demanded by his being – and that it is therefore intended by God in the same way as everything else about salvation. Hence, it will not be possible in any way to draw the conclusion from this conception that, since man is already an anonymous Christian even without it, this explicit preaching of Christianity is superfluous. Such a conclusion would be just as false (and for the same reasons) as to conclude that the sacraments of baptism and penance could be dispensed with because a person can be justified by his subjective acts of faith and contrition even before the reception of these sacraments.

The reflex self-realization of a previously anonymous Christianity is demanded (1) by the incarnational and social structure of grace and of Christianity, and (2) because the individual who grasps Christianity in a clearer, purer and more reflective way has, other things being equal, a still greater chance of salvation than someone who is merely an anonymous Christian. If, however, the message of the Church is directed to someone who is a 'non-Christian' only in the sense of living by an anonymous Christianity not as yet fully conscious of itself, then her missionary work must take this fact into account and must draw the necessary conclusions when deciding on its missionary strategy and tactics. We may say at a guess that this is still not the case in sufficient measure. The exact meaning of all this, however, cannot be developed further here.

4th Thesis: It is possibly too much to hope, on the one hand, that the religious pluralism which exists in the concrete situation of Christians will disappear in the foreseeable future. On the other hand, it is nevertheless absolutely permissible for the Christian himself to interpret this non-Christianity as Christianity of an anonymous kind which he does always still go out to meet as a missionary, seeing it as a world which is to be brought to the explicit consciousness of what already belongs to it as a divine offer or already pertains to it also over and above this as a divine gift of grace accepted unreflectedly and implicitly. If both these statements are true, then the Church will not so much regard herself today as the exclusive community of those who have a claim to salvation but rather as the historically tangible vanguard and the historically and socially constituted explicit expression of what the Christian hopes is present as a hidden reality even outside the visible Church.

To begin with, however much we must always work, suffer and pray anew and indefatigably for the unification of the whole human race, in the one Church of Christ, we must nevertheless expect, for theological reasons and not merely by reason of a profane historical analysis, that the religious pluralism existing in the world and in our own historical sphere of existence will not disappear in the foreseeable future. We know from the gospel that the opposition to Christ and to the Church will not disappear until the end of time. If anything, we must even be prepared for a heightening of this antagonism to Christian existence. If, however, this opposition to the Church cannot confine itself merely to the purely private sphere of the individual but must also be of a public, historical character, and if this opposition is said to be present in a history which today, in contrast to previous ages, possesses a worldwide unity, then the continuing opposition to the Church can no longer exist merely locally and outside a certain limited sector of history such as that of the West. It must be found in our vicinity and everywhere else. And this is part of what the Christian must expect and must learn to endure. The Church, which is at the same time the homogeneous characterization of an in itself homogeneous culture (i.e. the medieval Church), will no longer exist if history can no longer find any way to escape from or go back on the period of its planetary unity. In a unified world history in which everything enters into the life of everyone, the 'necessary' public opposition to Christianity is a factor in the existential sphere of all Christianity. If this Christianity, thus always faced with opposition and unable to expect seriously that this will ever cease, nevertheless believes in God's universal salvific will – in other words, believes that God can be victorious by his secret grace even where the Church does not win the victory but is contradicted – then this Church cannot feel herself to be just *one* dialectic moment in the whole of history but has already overcome this opposition by her faith, hope and charity. In other words, the others who oppose her are merely those who have not yet recognized what they nevertheless really already are (or can be) even when, on the surface of existence, they are in opposition; they are already anonymous Christians, and the Church is not the communion of those who possess God's grace as opposed to those who lack it, but is the communion of those who can explicitly confess what they *and* the others hope to be. Non-Christians may think it presumption for the Christian to judge everything which is sound or restored (by being sanctified) to be the fruit in every man of the grace of his Christ, and to interpret it as anonymous Christianity; they may think it presumption for the Christion to regard the non-Christian as a Christian who has not yet come to himself reflectively. But the Christian cannot renounce this 'presumption' which is really the source of the greatest humility both for himself and for the Church. For it is a profound admission of the fact that God is greater than man and the Church. The Church will go out to meet the non-Christian of tomorrow with the attitude expressed by St Paul when he said: What therefore you do not know and yet worship [and yet *worship*!] that I proclaim to you (Acts 17:23). On such a basis one can be tolerant, humble and yet firm towards all non-Christian religions.

4. DECLARATION ON THE RELATION OF THE CHURCH TO NON-CHRISTIAN RELIGIONS

Vatican II
(1965)

INTRODUCTION

In this age when the human race is daily becoming more closely united and ties between different peoples are becoming stronger, the Church considers more closely her own relation to non-Christian religions. Since it is her task to foster unity and love among men, and indeed among nations, she first considers in this declaration what men have in common and what draws them into fellowship together.

For, since God made all races of men and gave them the whole earth to inhabit (cf. Acts 17:26), all nations form a single community with a common origin; they also have a single final end which is God. God's providence and his evident goodness and his plan of salvation extend to all men (cf. Wisdom 8:1; Acts 14:17; Romans 2:6–7; 1 Timothy 2:4), until the time when all the elect are made one in the holy city, where all nations will walk in the brightness of God's glory which will be its light (cf. Apocalypse 21:23 ff.).

From his different religions, man seeks the answer to the riddles and problems of human existence; these exercise him no less deeply today than in the past: What is man? What is the meaning and purpose of life? What are goodness and sin? What is the origin and purpose of suffering?

Which is the way to attain true happiness? What is death, judgement and reward after death? What, lastly, is that ultimate and indescribable mystery, embracing the whole of our existence, which is both our origin and our end?

VARIOUS NON-CHRISTIAN RELIGIONS

From ancient times down to the present day there is found in various peoples a certain recognition of that hidden power which is present in history and human affairs, and in fact sometimes an acknowledgement of a supreme Godhead, or even of a Father. This recognition and acknowledgement give those people's lives a deep and pervading religious sense. With the advance of the civilizations with which they are connected, these religions endeavour to use more refined concepts and more developed language to answer these questions. Thus in Hinduism, men probe the mystery of God and express it with a rich fund of myths and a penetrating philosophy. They seek liberation from the constrictions of this world by various forms of asceticism, deep meditation or loving and trustful recourse to God. In the various forms of Buddhism the basic inadequacy of this changing world is recognized and men are taught how with confident application they can achieve a state of complete liberation, or reach the highest level of illumination, either through their own efforts or with help from above. There are other religions too, all over the world, which try to alleviate in various ways the anxieties of man's heart. To this end they put forward various 'ways' – doctrines and moral teaching as well as sacred rites.

The Catholic Church rejects nothing which is true and

holy in these religions. She has a sincere respect for those ways of acting and living, those moral and doctrinal teachings which may differ in many respects from what she holds and teaches, but which none the less often reflect the brightness of that Truth which is the light of all men. But she proclaims, and is bound to proclaim unceasingly, Christ, who is 'the way, the truth, and the life' (John 14:6). In him men find the fullness of their religious life and in him God has reconciled all things to himself (cf. 2 Corinthians 5:18–19).

She therefore urges her sons, using prudence and charity, to join members of other religions in discussions and collaboration. While bearing witness to their own Christian faith and life, they must acknowledge those good spiritual and moral elements and social and cultural values found in other religions, and preserve and encourage them.

ISLAM

The Church also regards with esteem the Muslims who worship the one, subsistent, merciful and almighty God, the Creator of heaven and earth, who has spoken to man. Islam willingly traces its descent back to Abraham, and just as he submitted himself to God, the Muslims endeavour to submit themselves to his mysterious decrees. They venerate Jesus as a prophet, without, however, recognizing him as God, and they pay honour to his virgin mother Mary and sometimes also invoke her with devotion. Further, they expect a day of judgement when God will raise all men from the dead and reward them. For this reason they attach importance to the moral life and worship God, mainly by prayer, alms-giving and fasting.

If in the course of the centuries there has arisen not

infrequent dissension and hostility between Christian and Muslim, this sacred Council now urges everyone to forget the past, to make sincere efforts at mutual understanding and to work together in protecting and promoting for the benefit of all men, social justice, good morals as well as peace and freedom.

THE JEWISH RELIGION

Probing the mystery of the Church, this sacred Council remembers the bond by which the people of the New Testament are spiritually linked to the line of Abraham.

The Church of Christ recognizes that in God's plan of salvation, the beginning of her own election and faith are to be found in the Patriarchs, Moses and the Prophets. She fully acknowledges that all believers in Christ, who are Abraham's sons in faith (cf. Galatians 3 : 7), are included in Abraham's calling and that the salvation of the Church is mystically prefigured in the exodus of the chosen people from the land of their bondage. The Church cannot, therefore, forget that it was through that people, with whom God in his ineffable mercy saw fit to establish the Old Covenant, that she herself has received the revelation of the Old Testament. She takes her nourishment from the root of the cultivated olive tree on to which the wild-olive branches of the Gentiles have been grafted (cf. Romans 11 : 17–24). The Church believes that Christ, who is our Peace, has reconciled Jews and Gentiles through the Cross and has made us both one in himself (cf. Ephesians 2 : 14–16).

The Church also always keeps before her eyes the words of the Apostle Paul concerning his kinsmen 'to whom belongeth the adoption as of children, and the glory, and the testament, and the giving of the law and the service of God and the promises: whose are the fathers, and of whom is Christ, according to the flesh' (Romans 9:4–5), the son of the Virgin Mary. She recalls too that the apostles, the foundations and pillars of the Church and very many of those first disciples who proclaimed the Gospel of Christ to the world, were born of the Jewish people.

Holy Scripture is witness that Jerusalem has not known the time of her visitation (cf. Luke 19:44). The Jews have not, for the most part, accepted the gospel; some indeed have opposed its diffusion (cf. Romans 11:28). Even so, according to the Apostle Paul, the Jews still remain very dear to God, for the sake of their fathers, since he does not repent of the gifts he makes or the calls he issues (cf. Romans 11:28–9). In company with the Prophets and the same Apostle, the Church looks forward to that day, known to God alone, when all peoples will call on the Lord with one voice and 'serve him with one shoulder' (Soph. 3:9; cf. Isaiah 66:23; Psalm 65:4; Romans 11:11–32).

Given this great spiritual heritage common to Christians and Jews, it is the wish of this sacred Council to foster and recommend a mutual knowledge and esteem, which will come from biblical and theological studies, and brotherly discussions.

Even if the Jewish authorities, together with their followers, urged the death of Christ (cf. John 19:6), what was done to him in his passion cannot be blamed on all Jews living at that time indiscriminately, or on the Jews of today. Although the Church is the new People of God, the Jews should not be presented as rejected by God or accursed, as though this followed from Scripture. Therefore all must take care that in instruction and in preaching the Word of God, they do not teach anything which is not in complete agreement with the truth of the Gospel and the spirit of Christ.

Further, the Church condemns all persecutions of any men; she remembers her common heritage with the Jews and, acting not from any political motives, but rather from a spiritual and evangelical love, deplores all hatred, persecutions and other manifestations of antisemitism, whatever the period and whoever was responsible.

But Christ, the Church holds and always has held, in his infinite love, underwent his passion and death voluntarily for the sins of all men in order that all might achieve salvation. It is the task of the Church in its preaching to proclaim the cross of Christ as a sign of God's universal love and as the source of all grace.

ANY SORT OF DISCRIMINATION EXCLUDES UNIVERSAL BROTHERHOOD

We cannot call on God, the Father of all men, if there are any men whom we refuse to treat as brothers, since all men are created in God's image. Man's relation to God the Father is connected with his relation to his fellow men in such a way that Scripture says 'He that loveth not, knoweth not God' (1 John 4:8).

There remain, then, no grounds for any theory or practice which leads to discrimination between men or races in matters concerning the dignity of man, and the rights which stem from it.

Therefore the Church condemns all discrimination between men and all conflict of race, colour, class or creed, as being contrary to the mind of Christ. Accordingly, following in the footsteps of the Apostles Peter and Paul, this sacred Council earnestly appeals to believers in Christ to 'conduct themselves well among the Gentiles' (1 Peter 2:12) if possible, and do their best to be at peace with all men (cf. Romans 12:18), so that they may be true sons of the Father who is in heaven (cf. Matthew 5:45).

5. THE CHRISTIAN IN A RELIGIOUSLY PLURAL WORLD

Wilfred Cantwell Smith

We live, if I may coin a phrase, in a time of transition. The observation is a platitude; but the transitions themselves through which we are moving, the radical transformations in which we find ourselves involved, are far from hackneyed. Rather, there is excitement and at times almost terror in the newness to which all our cherished past is giving way. In area after area we are becoming conscious of being participants in a process, where we thought we were carriers of a pattern.

I wish to attempt to discern and to delineate something at least of the momentous current that, if I mistake not, has begun to flow around and through the Christian Church. It is a current which, although we are only beginning to be aware of it, is about to become a flood that could sweep us quite away unless we can through greatly increased consciousness of its force and direction learn to swim in its special and mighty surge.

I refer to the movement that, had the word 'ecumenical' not been appropriated lately to designate rather an internal development within the on-going Church, might well have been called by that name, in its literal meaning of a world-wide humanity. I mean the emergence of a true cosmopolitanism, or according to the wording of my title, the Christian Church in a religiously plural world, which of course is the only world there is. Like the other, *the* 'ecumenical' movement, this transformation, too, begins at the frontier, on the mission field, the active confrontation of the Church with mankind's other faiths, other religious traditions. We shall begin there, too, but shall presently see that the issues raised cannot be left out there in the distance. They penetrate back into the scholar's study, and pursue us into what we were brought up to think of as the most intimate and most sanctified recesses of our theological traditions.

Regarding the missionary movement itself, I shall begin by stating quite bluntly and quite vigorously: the missionary enterprise is in profound and fundamental crisis. There has been some temptation to recognize this more on the practical than on the theoretical level. There has been some temptation, perhaps, even not to recognize it at all! – or at least, not to recognize how serious, and how far-reaching, it is: that the whole Church is involved, and not merely 'those interested in missions'.

At the practical level the situation is acute enough. It is not only in China that the traditional missionary venture has come or is coming to an end. Take the problem of recruitment: more have remarked on the fact that volunteers today are either scarce or curious, than that today no mission board can in fact offer any young person a life vocation on the mission field. Since some persons in the Church at home seem not to realize the kind of feeling on these matters to be found in the non-Western world, I shall quote from the report of a Christian Missionary Activities Enquiry Committee appointed in 1954 by the state government of Madhya Pradesh in India. Among its recommendations were the following:

> Those missionaries whose primary object is proselytization should be asked to withdraw. The large influx of foreign missionaries is undesirable and should be checked . . .

> The use of medical or other professional service as a direct means of making conversions should be prohibited by law . . .
>
> Any attempt by force or fraud, or threats of illicit means or grants of financial or other aid, or by fraudulent means or promises, or by moral and material assistance, or by taking advantage of any person's inexperience or confidence, or by exploiting any person's necessity, spiritual (mental) weakness or thoughtlessness, or, in general, any attempt or effort (whether successful or not), directly or indirectly to penetrate into the religious conscience of persons (whether of age or underage) of another faith, for the purpose of consciously altering their religious conscience or faith, so as to agree with the ideas or convictions of the proselytizing party should be absolutely prohibited . . .
>
> An amendment of the Constitution of India may be sought, firstly, to clarify that the right of propagation has been given only to the citizens of India and secondly, that it does not include conversions brought about by force, fraud, or other illicit means.[1]

China, Angola, the Arab world after Suez, this sort of attitude in India, and the like are not simply illustrations of a practical problem. They are symptoms of an intellectual, emotional, and spiritual problem in which Christians are involved. Few Western Christians have any inkling of the involvement of the Church within the object of anti-Westernism, or of the religious involvement of the resurgence in Asia and Africa of other communities. Of this resurgence we see usually only the political or economic facets, because these are the only ones that we can understand. The religious history of mankind is taking as monumental a turn in our century as is the political or economic, if only we could see it. And the upsurge of a vibrant and self-assertive new religious orientation of Buddhists and Hindus and the like evinces a new phase not merely in the history of those particular traditions, but in the history of the whole complex of man's religiousness, of which the Christian is a part, and an increasingly participant part. The traditional relation of the Christian Church to man's other religious traditions has been that of proselytizing evangelism, at least in theory. The end of that phase is the beginning of a new phase, in which the relation of the Church to other faiths will be new. But what it will be, in theory or practice, has yet to be worked out – not by the Church alone, but by the Church in its involvement with these others.

The missionary situation of the Church, then, is in profound crisis, in both practice and theory. The most vivid and most masterly summing up of this crisis is perhaps the brief remark of Canon Max Warren, the judicious and brilliant and sensitive and responsible General Secretary in London of the Church Missionary Society. His obituary on traditional mission policy and practice is in three sentences: 'We have marched around alien Jerichos the requisite number of times. We have sounded the trumpets. And the walls have not collapsed.'

We come back from the mission field to North America, and to theology. Traditional missions are the exact extrapolation of the traditional theology of the Church. The passing of traditional missions is a supersession of one phase of the Church's traditional theology. The 'ecumenical' movements have been the result in part of pressures from the mission field because there the scandal of a divided Christendom came most starkly to light. It is from the mission field also that the scandal of a fundamental fallacy in traditional theology has been shown up.

The rise of science in the nineteenth century induced a revision in Christian theology – what has sometimes been called the second Reformation. Some may think that Canon Warren exaggerates, but at least he calls attention to the seriousness of the new challenge, when he says that the impact of agnostic science will turn out to have been as child's play compared to the challenge to Christian theology of the faith of other men.[2]

The woeful thing is that the meeting of that challenge has hardly seriously begun.

An illuminating story was told me by a Harvard friend, concerning Paul Tillich. Apparently a letter in the student paper, the *Harvard Crimson*, was able to show up as superficial in a particular case this eminent theologian's understanding of religious traditions in Asia. Some would perhaps find it not particularly surprising that an undergraduate these days should know more on this matter than a major Christian thinker. Until recently, certainly, it was not particularly expected that a man should know much, or indeed anything, about the religious life of other communities before he undertook to become a spokesman for his own. To me, however, the incident raises a significant issue. Looking at the matter historically, one may perhaps put it thus: probably Tillich belongs to the last generation of theologians who can formulate their conceptual system as religiously isolationist. The era of religious isolationism is about to be as much at an end as that of political isolationism already is. The pith of Tillich's exposition has to do with its deliberate aptness to the intellectual context in which it appears: the correlation technique, of question and answer. But that context as he sees it is the mental climate of the Western world; and he has spoken to it just at the end of its separatist tradition, just before it is superseded by a new context, a climate modified radically by new breezes, or new storms, blowing in from the other parts of the planet. The new generation of the Church, unless it is content with a ghetto, will live in a cosmopolitan environment, which will make the work of even a Tillich appear parochial.[3]

Ever since the impact of Greek philosophy on the Church, or shall we say the forced discovery of Greek philosophy by the Church, in the early centuries, every Christian theology has been written in the light of it. Whether the Christian thinker rejected or accepted it, modified or enriched it, he formulated his exposition aware of it, and aware that his readers would read him in the light of it. No serious intellectual statement of the Christian faith since that time has ignored this conceptual context.

Similarly, ever since the rise of science, the forced discovery of science by the Church, again subsequent Christian doctrine has been written in the light of it. Formulator and reader are aware of this context, and no intellectual statement that ignores it can be fully serious.

I suggest that we are about to enter a comparable situation with regard to the other religious traditions of mankind. The time will soon be with us when a theologian who attempts to work out his position unaware that he does so as a member of a world society in which other theologians equally intelligent, equally devout, equally moral, are Hindus, Buddhists, Muslims, and unaware that his readers are likely perhaps to be Buddhists or to have Muslim husbands or Hindu colleagues – such a theologian is as out of date as is one who attempts to construct an intellectual position unaware that Aristotle has thought about the world or that existentialists have raised new orientations, or unaware that the earth is a minor planet in a galaxy that is vast only by terrestrial standards.

Philosophy and science have impinged so far on theological thought more effectively than has comparative religion, but this will not last.

It is not my purpose in this essay to suggest the new theological systems that the Church will in the new situation bring forth. My task is to delineate the problems that such a system must answer, to try to analyse the context within which future theological thought will inescapably be set. Intellectually, we have had or are having our Copernican Revolution, but not yet our Newton. By this I mean that we have discovered the facts of our earth's being one of the planets, but have not yet explained them. The pew, if not yet the pulpit, the undergraduate if not yet the seminary professor, have begun to recognize not only that the Christian answers on man's cosmic quality are not the only answers, but even that the Christian questions are not the only questions. The awareness of multiformity is becoming vivid, and compelling.

Before Newton's day it used to be thought that we live in a radically dichotomous universe: there was our earth, where things fell to the ground, and there were the heavens, where things went round in circles. These were two quite different realms, and one did not think of confusing or even much relating the two. A profoundly significant step was taken when men recognized that the apple and the moon are in much the same kind of motion. Newton's mind was able to conceive an interpretation – accepted now by all of us, but revolutionary at the time – that without altering the fact that on earth things *do* fall to the ground and in the heavens things *do* go round in circles, yet saw both these facts as instances of a single kind of behaviour. In the religious field, the academic approach is similarly restless at the comparable dichotomy that for each group has in the past seen *our* tradition (whichever it be) as faith, other men's behaviour as superstition, the two realms to be explained in quite unrelated ways, understood on altogether separate principles. The Christian's faith has come down from God, the Buddhist's goes round and round in the circles of purely human aspiration, and so on. The intellectual challenge here is to make coherent sense, in a rational, integrated manner, of a wide range of apparently comparable and yet conspicuously diverse phenomena. And the academic world is closer to meeting this challenge than some theologians have noticed.

Certain Christians have even made the rather vigorous assertion that the Christian faith is *not* one of 'the religions of the world', that one misunderstands it if one attempts to see it in those terms. Most students of comparative religion have tended to pooh-pooh such a claim as unacceptable. I, perhaps surprisingly, take it very seriously indeed but I have discovered that the same applies to the other traditions also. The Christian faith is not to be seen as a religion, one of the religions. But neither is the faith of Buddhists, Hindus, Muslims or Andaman Islanders; and to think of it so is seriously to misunderstand and distort it. This is a large issue that I have treated in my book *The Meaning and End of Religion.* I believe there is no question but that modern enquiry is showing that other men's faith is not so different from ours as we were brought up to suppose.

Religious diversity poses a general human problem because it disrupts community. It does so with new force in the modern world because divergent traditions that in the past did and could develop separately and insouciantly are today face to face; and, perhaps even more important and radical, are for the first time side by side. Different civilizations have in the past either ignored each other or fought each other; very occasionally in tiny ways perhaps they met each other. Today they not only meet but interpenetrate; they meet not only each other, but jointly meet joint problems, and must jointly try to solve them. They must collaborate. Perhaps the single most important challenge that mankind faces in our day is the need to turn our nascent world society into a world community.

This is not easy. Men have yet to learn our new task of living together as partners in a world of religious and cultural plurality. The technological and economic aspects of 'one world', of a humanity in process of global integration, are proceeding apace, and at the least are receiving the attention of many of our best minds and most influential groups. The political aspects also are under active and constant consideration, even though success here is not so evident, except in the supremely important day-to-day staving off of disaster. The ideological and cultural question of human cohesion, on the other hand, has received little attention, and relatively little progress can be reported, even though in the long run it may prove utterly crucial, and is already basic to much else. Unless men can learn to understand and to be loyal to each other across religious frontiers, unless we can build a world in which people profoundly of different faiths can live together and work together, then the prospects for our planet's future are not bright.

My own view is that the task of constructing even that minimum degree of world fellowship that will be necessary for man to survive at all is far too great to be accomplished on any other than a religious basis. From no other source than his faith, I believe, can man muster the energy, devotion, vision, resolution, the capacity to survive disappointment, that will be necessary – that *are* necessary – for this challenge. Co-operation among men of diverse religion is a moral imperative, even at the lowest level of social and political life.

Some would agree that the world community must have a religious basis, conceding that a lasting and peaceful society cannot be built by a group of men that are ultimately divided religiously, that have come to no mutual understanding; but would go on to hold that this is possible only if their own one tradition prevails. No doubt to some it would seem nice if all men were Roman Catholics, or Communists, or liberal universalists; or if all men would agree that religion does not really matter, or that it should be kept a private affair. Apart, however, from those that find such a vision inherently less appealing, many others will agree that for the moment it seems in any case hardly likely. Co-existence, if not a final truth of man's diversity, would seem at least an immediate necessity, and indeed, an immediate virtue.

If we must have rivalry among the religious communities of earth, might we not for the moment at least rival each other in our determination and capacity to promote reconciliation? Christians, Muslims and Buddhists each believe that only *they* are able to do this. Rather than arguing this point ideologically, let us strive in a friendly race to see which can implement it most effectively and vigorously in practice – each recognizing that any success of the other is to be applauded, not decried.

We may move from the general human level to the specifically Christian level. Here I have something very special to adduce. It is a thesis that I have been trying to develop, and is essentially this: that the emergence of the new world situation has brought to light a lack of integration in one area of Christian awareness, namely between the moral and the intellectual facets of our relations with our fellow men.

I begin with the affirmation that there are moral as well

as conceptual implications of revealed truth. If we take seriously the revelation of God in Christ – if we really mean what we say when we affirm that his life, and his death on the cross, and his final triumph out of the very midst of self-sacrifice, embody the ultimate truth and power and glory of the universe – then two kinds of things follow, two orders of inference. On the moral level, there follows an imperative towards reconciliation, unity, harmony and brotherhood. At this level, all men are included: we strive to break down barriers, to close up gulfs; we recognize all men as neighbours, as fellows, as sons of the universal father, seeking him and finding him, being sought by him and being found by him. At this level, we do not become truly Christian until we have reached out towards a community that turns mankind into one total 'we'.

On the other hand, there is another level, the intellectual, the order of ideas, where it is the business of those of us who are theologians to draw out concepts, to construct doctrines. At this level, the doctrines that Christians have traditionally derived have tended to affirm a Christian exclusivism, a separation between those who believe and those who do not, a division of mankind into a 'we' and a 'they', a gulf between Christendom and the rest of the world: a gulf profound, ultimate, cosmic.

I shall come to the theological consideration of these theological ideas in the last part of this essay. At the moment, I wish to consider the moral consequences of our theological ideas. Here my submission is that on this front the traditional doctrinal position of the Church has in fact militated against its traditional moral position, and has in fact encouraged Christians to approach other men immorally. Christ has taught us humility, but we have approached them with arrogance.

I do not say this lightly. This charge of arrogance is a

serious one. It is my observation over more than twenty years of study of the Orient, and a little now of Africa, that the fundamental flaw of Western civilization in its role in world history is arrogance, and that this has infected also the Christian Church. If you think that I am being reckless or unwarranted here, ask any Jew, or read between the lines of the works of modern African or Asian thinkers.

May I take for illustration a phrase, not unrepresentative, which was under discussion recently by the United Church of Canada's commission on faith, and which ran as follows: 'Without the particular knowledge of God in Jesus Christ, men do not really know God at all.' Let us leave aside for the moment any question of whether or not this is true. We shall return to that presently. My point here is simply that, in any case, it is arrogant. At least, it becomes arrogant when one carries it out to the non-Western world. In the quiet of the study, it may be possible for the speculative mind to produce this kind of doctrine, provided that one keep it purely bookish. But except at the cost of insensitivity or delinquence, it is morally not possible actually to go out into the world and say to devout, intelligent, fellow human beings: 'We are saved and you are damned', or, 'We believe that we know God, and we are right; you believe that you know God, and you are totally wrong.'

This is intolerable from merely human standards. It is doubly so from Christian ones. Any position that antagonizes and alienates rather than reconciles, that is arrogant rather than humble, that promotes segregation rather than brotherhood, that is unlovely, is *ipso facto* un-Christian.

There is a further point at which the traditional position seems to me morally un-Christian. From the notion that if Christianity is true, then other religions must be false (a notion whose logic I shall challenge later), it is possible to go on to the converse proposition: that if anyone else's faith turns out to be valid or adequate, then it would follow that Christianity must be false – a form of logic that has, in fact, driven many from their own faith, and indeed from any faith at all. If one's chances of getting to Heaven – or to use a nowadays more acceptable metaphor, of coming into God's presence – are dependent upon other people's not getting there, then one becomes walled up within the quite intolerable position that the Christian has a vested interest in other men's damnation. It is shocking to admit it, but this actually takes place. When an observer comes back from Asia, or from a study of Asian religious traditions, and reports that, contrary to accepted theory, some Hindus and Buddhists and some Muslims lead a pious and moral life and seem very near to God by any possible standards, so that, so far as one can see, in these particular cases at least faith is as 'adequate' as Christian faith, then presumably a Christian should be overjoyed, enthusiastically hopeful that this be true, even though he might be permitted a fear lest it not be so. Instead, I have sometimes witnessed just the opposite: an emotional resistance to the news, men hoping firmly that it is not so, though perhaps with a covert fear that it might be. Whatever the rights and wrongs of the situation theoretically, I submit that practically this is just not Christian, and indeed is not tolerable. It will not do, to have a faith that can be undermined by God's saving one's neighbour; or to be afraid lest other men turn out to be closer to God than one had been led to suppose.

Let us turn, finally, to the theological problem, which the existence of other religious communities poses for the Christian (and that today's new immediate and face-to-face awareness of their existence poses urgently). This problem began, in a compelling form, with the discovery of America, and the concomitant discovery of men on this continent who had been 'out of reach of the Gospel'. In theory the peoples of Africa and Asia could have heard the Gospel story and could have believed it and been saved. If they had not become Christian, this could be interpreted as due to their cussedness, or to Christian lethargy in not evangelizing them, and so on. But with the discovery of 'redskins' in America who had lived for fifteen centuries since Christ died, unable to be saved through faith in him, many sensitive theologians were bewildered.

In our day a comparable problem is presented, and may be viewed in two ways. First, how does one account, theologically, for the fact of man's religious diversity? This is really as big an issue, almost, as the question of how one accounts theologically for evil – but Christian theologians have been much more conscious of the fact of evil than that of religious pluralism. Another way of viewing it is to phrase a question as to whether or how far or how non-Christians are saved, or know God. The diversity question has got, so far as I know, almost no serious answers of any kind. The latter has found a considerable number of attempted answers, though to my taste none of these is at all satisfactory.

On the former point I would simply like to suggest that from now on any serious intellectual statement of the Christian faith must include, if it is to serve its purpose among men, some sort of doctrine of other religions. We explain the fact that the Milky Way is there by the doctrine of creation, but how do we explain the fact that the *Bhagavad Gita* is there?

This would presumably include also an answer to our second question. Here I would like merely to comment on one of the answers that have in fact been given. It is the one that we have already mentioned: 'Without the particular knowledge of God in Jesus Christ, men do not really know God at all.' First, of course, one must recognize the positive point that this intellectualization stems from and attempts to affirm the basic and ultimate and of course positive faith of the Church that in Christ God died for us men and our salvation, that through faith in him we are saved. In the new formulations to which we may look forward, this positive faith must be preserved. Yet in the negative proposition as framed, one may see a number of difficulties, and one may suppose that the force of these will come to be increasingly felt in coming decades.

First, there is an epistemological difficulty. How could one possibly know?

If one asks how we know the Christian faith to be true, there are perhaps two kinds of answer. First, we ourselves find in our lives, by accepting and interiorizing and attempting to live in accordance with it, that it proves itself. We know it to be true because we have lived it. Secondly, one may answer that for now almost two thousand years the Church has proven it and found it so – hundreds of millions of people, of all kinds and in all circumstances and in many ages, have staked their lives upon it, and have found it right. On the other hand, if one is asked how one knows the faith of people in other traditions to be false, one is rather stumped.

Most people who make this kind of statement do not in fact know much about the matter. Actually the only basis on which their position can and does rest is a logical inference. It seems to them a theoretical implication of what they themselves consider to be true, that other people's faith *must* be illusory. Personally, I think that this is to put far too much weight on logical implication. There have been innumerable illustrations of man's capacity for starting from some cogent theoretical position and then inferring from it logically something else that at the time seems to him persuasive but that in fact turns out on practical investigation not to hold. It is far too sweeping to condemn the great majority of mankind to lives of utter meaninglessness and perhaps to hell, simply on the basis of what seems to some individuals the force of logic. Part of what the Western world has been doing for the last four centuries has been learning to get away from this kind of reliance on purely logical structures, totally untested by experience or by any other consideration. The damnation of my neighbour is too weighty a matter to rest on a syllogism.

Secondly, there is the problem of empirical observation. One cannot be anything but tentative here, of course, and inferential. Yet so far as actual observation goes, the evidence would seem overwhelming that in fact individual Buddhists, Hindus, Muslims and others have known, and do know, God. I personally have friends from these communities whom it seems to me preposterous to think about in any other way. (If we do not have friends among these communities, we should probably refrain from generalizations about them.)

This point, however, presumably need not be laboured. The position set forth has obviously not been based, and does not claim to be based, upon empirical observation. If one insists on holding it, it must be held *against* the evidence of empirical observation. This can be done, as a recent writer has formulated it:

> The Gospel of Jesus Christ comes to us with a built-in prejudgement of all other faiths so that we know in advance of our study what we must ultimately conclude about them. They give meanings to life apart from that

> which God has given in the biblical story culminating with Jesus Christ, and they organize life outside the covenant community of Jesus Christ. Therefore, devoid of this saving knowledge and power of God, these faiths not only are unable to bring men to God, they actually lead men away from God and hold them captive from God. This definitive and blanket judgement . . . is not derived from our investigation of the religions but is given in the structure and content of Gospel faith itself.[4]

Again, a careful study by a neo-orthodox trainer of missionaries in Basle, Dr Emanuel Kellerhals, says that Islam, like other 'foreign religions', is a 'human attempt to win God for oneself . . . to catch Him and confine Him on the plane of one's own spiritual life . . . and for oneself to hold Him fast'.[5] He knows this, he says explicitly, not from a study of Islam but before he begins that study, from his Christian premises; he knows it by revelation, and therefore he can disdain all human argument against it. The position seems thoroughly logical, and once one has walled oneself up within it, impregnable. Those of us who, *after* our study of Islam or Indian or Chinese religion, and after our fellowship with Muslims and other personal friends, have come to know that these religious traditions are not that, but are channels through which God himself comes into touch with these his children – what answer can we give?

One possible answer is that empirical knowledge does in the end have to be reckoned with, does in the end win out even over conviction that claims for itself the self-certification of revelation. We do not deny that upholders of this sort of position are recipients of revelation, genuinely; but we would argue that the revelation itself is not propositional, and that their interpretation of the revelation that they have received is their own, is human and fallible, is partial, and in this case is in some ways wrong.

In fact, we have been through all this before. A hundred years ago the Christian argued that he knew by divine revelation that the earth was but six thousand years old and that evolution did not happen, and therefore any evidence that geologists or biologists might adduce to the contrary need not be taken seriously. A repentant Church still claims revelation but now admits that its former theology needed revision. In the twentieth century the increasing evidence that the faith of men in other religious communities is not so different from our own as we have traditionally asserted it to be, although it is forcing some to abandon any faith in revelation at all, will in general, we predict, force us, rather, to revise our theological formulations.

Finally, even on the side of internal Christian doctrine the exclusivist position is theoretically difficult. For according to traditional Christian doctrine, there is not only one person in the Trinity, namely Christ, but three persons: God the Father, God the Son, and God the Holy Spirit. Is God not Creator? If so, then is he not to be known – however impartially, distortedly, inadequately – in creation? Is he not active in history? If so, is his spirit totally absent from any history, including even the history of other men's faith?

It may be argued that outside the Christian tradition men may know God in part, but cannot know him fully. This is undoubtedly valid, but the apparent implications are perhaps precarious. For one may well ask: is it possible for a Christian to know God fully? I personally do not see what it might mean to say that any man, Christian or other, has a complete knowledge of God. This would certainly be untenable this side of the grave, at the very least. The finite cannot comprehend the infinite.

What does one actually mean when one speaks of the knowledge of God? It has been said, and I think rightly, that the only true atheist is he who loves no one and whom no one loves, who is blind to all beauty and all justice, who knows no truth, and who has lost all hope.

Christians know God only in part. But one part of their knowing him is the recognition that he does not leave any of us utterly outside his knowledge.

It is easier, however, of course, to demolish a theological position than to construct an alternative one. The fallacy of relentless exclusivism is becoming more obvious than is the right way of reconciling a truly Christian charity and perceptivity with doctrinal adequacy. On this matter I personally have a number of views, but the one about which I feel most strongly is that this matter is important – while the rest of my particular views on it are not necessarily so. In other words, I am much more concerned to stress the fact that the Church must work, and work vigorously, and work on a large scale, in order to construct an adequate doctrine in this realm (which in my view it has never yet elaborated), than I am concerned to push my own particular suggestions. Most of all I would emphasize that whether or not my particular construction seems inadequate, the position formulated above from which I strongly dissent must in any case be seen to be inadequate also.

Having expressed this caution, I may none the less make one or two suggestions. First, I rather feel that the final doctrine on this matter may perhaps run along the lines of affirming that a Buddhist who is saved, or a Hindu or a Muslim or whoever, is saved, and is saved only, because God is the kind of God whom Jesus Christ has revealed him to be. This is not exclusivist; indeed, it coheres, I feel, with the points that I have made above in dissenting from exclusivism. If the Christian revelation were *not* true, then it might be possible to imagine that God would allow Hindus to worship him or Muslims to obey him or Buddhists to feel compassionate towards their fellows, without his responding, without his reaching out to hold them in his arms. But because God is what he is, because he is what Christ has shown him to be, *therefore* other men *do* live in his presence. Also, therefore, we (as Christians) know this to be so.

I rather wonder whether the fundamental difficulty in the formulated position, and in all similar statements, does not arise somehow from an anthropocentric emphasis that it surreptitiously implies. To talk of man's knowing God is to move in the realm of thinking of religion as a human quest, and of knowledge of God as something that man attains, or even achieves. Of course it does not state it thus, but it skirts close to implying somehow that we are saved by *our* doings (or knowings). Must one not, rather, take the Christian doctrine of grace more seriously? The question must be more adequately phrased: Does God let himself be known only to those to whom he has let himself be known through Christ? Does God love only those who respond to him in this tradition?

We are not saved by our knowledge; we are not saved by our membership in the Church; we are not saved by anything of *our* doing. We are saved, rather, by the only thing that could possibly save us, the anguish and the love of God. While we have no final way of knowing with assurance how God deals or acts in other men's lives, and therefore cannot make any final pronouncement (such as the formulator of the position stated has attempted to make), none the less we must perhaps at least be hesitant in setting boundaries to that anguish and that love.

The God whom we have come to know, so far as we can sense his action, reaches out after all men everywhere, and speaks to all who will listen. Both within and without the Church men listen all too dimly. Yet both within and without the Church, so far as we can see, God does somehow enter into men's hearts.

1. As cited in Edmund Perry, *The Gospel in Dispute: The Relation of Christian Faith to Other Missionary Religions* New York, 1958, pp. 18f.
2. In an address at Scarborough, Ontario, 18 October 1958.
3. It is pleasant to report that after my remarks were first set forth Dr Tillich, having spent some time in Japan, published four lectures on *Christianity and the Encounter of the World Religions*, New York, 1963. [An extract from this book appears as Chapter 6 below.]
4. Perry, *The Gospel in Dispute*, p. 83.
5. Emanuel Kellerhals, *Der Islam: seine Geschichte, seine Lehre, sein Wesen*, second ed., Basle and Stuttgart, 1956, pp. 15f. Translation by Wilfred Cantwell Smith.

6. CHRISTIANITY JUDGING ITSELF IN THE LIGHT OF ITS ENCOUNTER WITH THE WORLD RELIGIONS

Paul Tillich

Under the general title, *Christianity and the Encounter of the World Religions,*[1] we gave first a view of the present situation, distinguishing between religions proper and secular quasi-religions. In drawing a map of their encounters all over the world we emphasized the fact that the most conspicuous encounters are those of the quasi-religions – Fascism, Communism, liberal humanism – with the primitive as well as the high religions, and that in consequence of this situation all religions have the common problem: how to encounter secularism and the quasi-religions based on it.

In the second chapter, under the title, 'Christian Principles of Judging Non-Christian Religions', we tried to show a long line of Christian universality affirming revelatory experiences in non-Christian religions, a line starting in the prophets and Jesus, carried on by the Church Fathers, interrupted for centuries by the rise of Islam and of Christian anti-Judaism, and taken up again in the Renaissance and the Enlightenment. This principle of universalism has been under continual attack by the opposite principle, that of particularity with the claim to exclusive validity, which has led to the unsettled and contradictory attitude of present-day Christianity towards the world religions. The same ambiguous attitude, we pointed out, is prevalent in the judgements of contemporary Christian leaders with respect to the quasi-religions and secularism generally.

In the third chapter, entitled 'A Christian-Buddhist Conversation', we discussed, first, the problem of a typology of religions and suggested the use of a dynamic typology, based on polarities instead of antitheses, as a way of understanding the seemingly chaotic history of religions. As a most important example of such polarity Christianity and Buddhism were confronted, points of convergence and divergence shown, and the whole summed up in the two contrasting symbols, Kingdom of God and Nirvana. The chapter ended with the question: how can a community of democratic nations be created without the religions out of which liberal democracy in the Western world originally arose?

The last question leads us to the subject of this chapter, 'Christianity Judging Itself in the Light of Its Encounters with the World Religions', meaning both religions proper and quasi-religions.

I

Let us consider first the basis of such self-judgement. Where does Christianity find its criteria? There is only one point from which the criteria can be derived and only one way to approach this point. The point is the event on which Christianity is based, and the way is the participation in the continuing spiritual power of this event, which is the appearance and reception of Jesus of Nazareth as the Christ, a symbol which stands for the decisive self-manifestation in human history of the source and aim of all being. This is the point from which the criteria of judging Christianity in the name of Christianity must be taken.

The way to this point is through participation, but how can one participate in an event of the past? Certainly not by historical knowledge, although we must listen to the witnesses to what happened; certainly not by acceptance of a tradition, although only through tradition can one be in living contact with the past; certainly not by subjecting oneself to authorities past or present, although there is no spiritual life without an actual (but not principal) dependence on authorities. Participation in an event of the past is only possible if one is grasped by the spiritual power of this event and through it is enabled to evaluate the witnesses, the traditions and the authorities in which the same spiritual power was and is effective.

It is possible, through participation, to discover in the appearance of the Christ in history the criteria by which Christianity must judge itself, but it is also possible to miss them. I am conscious of the fact that there is a risk involved, but where there is spirit, and not letter and law, there is always risk. This risk is unavoidable if one tries to judge Christianity in the name of its own foundation, but *if* it is done, it gives an answer to the question implied in the general subject of these lectures, 'Christianity and the Encounter of the World Religions'.

In the second chapter we discussed two tensions in the Christian self-interpretation, the first decisive for the relation of Christianity to the religions proper, and the second decisive for the relation of Christianity to the quasi-religions. The first is the tension between the particular and the universal character of the Christian claim; the second is the tension between Christianity as a religion and Christianity as the negation of religion. Both of these tensions follow from the nature of the event on which

Christianity is based. The meaning of this event shows not in its providing a foundation for a new religion with a particular character (though this followed, unavoidably, with consequences partly creative and partly destructive, ambiguously mixed in Church history), but it shows in the event itself, which preceded and judges these consequences. It is a personal life, the image of which, as it impressed itself on his followers, shows no break in his relation to God and no claim for himself in his particularity. What is particular in him is that he crucified the particular in himself for the sake of the universal. This liberates his image from bondage both to a particular religion – the religion to which he belonged has thrown him out – and to the religious sphere as such; the principle of love in him embraces the cosmos, including both the religious and the secular spheres. With this image, particular yet free from particularity, religious yet free from religion, the criteria are given under which Christianity must judge itself and, by judging itself, judge also the other religions and the quasi-religions.

II

On this basis Christianity has developed into a specific religion through a process of perpetuating the tradition of the Old Testament and, at the same time, of receiving elements from all the other confronted religions. As Harnack has said, Christianity in itself is a compendium of the history of religion. Although the first formative centuries were the most important in the whole development, the process has continued up to the present day. In it Christianity judged, was judged, and accepted judgement. The dynamic life it showed was nourished by the tension between judging the encountered religions in the strength of its foundation, and accepting judgement from them in the freedom its foundation gives. Christianity has in its very nature an openness in all directions, and for centuries this openness and receptivity was its glory. But there were two factors which limited more and more the freedom of Christianity to accept judgement: the hierarchical and the polemical. With the strengthening of the hierarchical authority it became increasingly difficult for it to recant or to alter decisions made by bishops, councils and, finally, Popes. The tradition ceased to be a living stream; it became an ever-augmented sum of immovably valid statements and institutions. But even more effective in this development was the polemical factor. Every important decision in the history of the Church is the solution of a problem raised by conflicts in history, and a decision, once made, cuts off other possibilities. It closes doors, it narrows down. It increases the proclivity to judge, and it decreases the willingness to accept judgement. The worst consequence of this tendency was the split of the Church in the period of the Reformation and the Counter-Reformation. After that the glory of openness was lost to both sides. The Church of the Counter-Reformation was incomparably less able to encounter the other religions or quasi-religions than the early Church had been, and in the Protestant churches, in spite of the freedom the Protestant principle gives, it was only the influence of secularism which again opened them to a creative encounter with other religions. One sometimes points to the skill with which missionaries, especially in Catholic orders, adapt their message and their demands to the pagan substance of a superficially converted group. But adaptation is not reception and does not lead to self-judgement. In the light of this consideration we must acknowledge the degree to which Christianity has become a religion instead of remaining a centre of crystallization for all positive religious elements after they have been subjected to the criteria implied in this centre. Much of the criticism directed against Christianity is due to this failure.

With this general view in mind I want now to give examples of the way in which Christianity both judged other religions and accepted judgement from them, and finally to show the inner-Christian struggle against itself as a religion, and the new vistas which open up in consequence of these struggles for the future encounters of Christianity with the world religions.

Strictly in the Jewish tradition, the early Christians judged polytheism as idolatry, or the service of demonic powers. This judgement was accompanied by anxiety and horror. Polytheism was felt to be a direct attack on the divinity of the divine, an attempt to elevate finite realities, however great and beautiful, to ultimacy in being and meaning. The glory of the Greek gods impressed the Christians as little as did the animal-shaped divinities of the 'barbaric' nations. But there arose a counterjudgement: the cultivated adherents of polytheistic symbolism accused the Jews and Christians of atheism, because they denied the divine presence in every realm of being. They were accused of profanizing the world. Somehow they were themselves aware of this fact. They did not moderate their abhorrence of polytheism, but they found many concrete manifestations of the divine in the world, for instance, hypostatized qualities or functions of God like his 'Wisdom' or his 'Word' or his 'Glory'. They saw in nature and history traces of angelic and demonic powers. Further – and in this Christianity parted ways with Judaism – they affirmed a divine mediator between God and man, and through him a host of saints and martyrs – mediators between the mediator and man, so to speak. In this respect Christianity has accepted influences from the polytheistic element of religion. In a secular form the conflict is alive even today as the conflict between a romantic philosophy of nature and its religious-artistic expression, on the one hand, and the total profanization of nature and its moral and technical subjection to man's purposes, on the other.

I have chosen this example of a most radical judgement of another religious type by Christianity, which yet did not prevent the Christians from accepting judgement from it in turn.

Although it is itself based on the Old Testament, Christianity judged and still judges Judaism, but because of its dependence upon it, is most inhibited from accepting judgement from it. Nevertheless, Christians have done so since the removal of the barriers of medieval suppression which was born of anxiety and fanaticism. For almost two hundred years Christianity, by way of liberal humanism, has received Jewish judgement indirectly and has transformed the critique into self-judgement. It was partly the resurgence of pagan elements in the national and territorial churches, and partly the suppression of the self-critical spirit in all churches, which called forth a prophetic reaction in democratic and socialist Christians.

I would like to be able to say more about judgement and the acceptance of judgement in relation to Islam, but there is little to say. The early encounter resulted only in mutual rejection. Are there possibilities for Christian self-judgement in these encounters? There are at two points – in the solution of the racial problem in Islam and in its wisdom in dealing with the primitive peoples. But this is probably all.

Another example of a radical rejection in connection with elements of acceptance was the dualistic religion of

Persia, introduced into Christianity by Gnostic groups and supported by the Greek doctrine of matter resisting the spirit. The fight against dualism and the rejection of a God of darkness with creative powers of his own were consequences of the Old Testament doctrine of creation. For this Christianity fought, but the Christians were, at the same time, impressed by the seriousness with which dualism took the problem of evil; Augustine was for this reason a Manichean for ten years. There are also many Christians today who, with Augustine and his Protestant followers up to Karl Barth, accept the 'total depravity' of man, a dualistic concept which was judged and accepted at the same time, and is being judged and accepted in present discussions for and against the existentialist view of man's predicament.

Christianity had encountered mysticism long before the modern opening up of India. A decisive struggle was made against Julian the Apostate's ideas of a restitution of paganism with the help of Neoplatonic mysticism. When we look at this struggle we find, on both sides, arguments similar to those used in our contemporary encounters with Indian mysticism. The Christian theologians were and are right in criticizing the nonpersonal, nonsocial and nonhistorical attitude of the mystical religions, but they had to accept the countercriticism of the mystical groups that their own personalism is primitive and needs interpretation in transpersonal terms. This has been at least partly accepted by Christian theologians who, in agreement with the long line of Christian mystics, have asserted that without a mystical element – namely, an experience of the immediate presence of the divine – there is no religion at all.

The examples could be multiplied, but these may suffice to illustrate the rhythm of criticism, countercriticism and self-criticism throughout the history of Christianity. They show that Christianity is not imprisoned in itself and that in all its radical judgements about other religions some degree of acceptance of counterjudgements took place.

III

We have discussed the judgement of Christianity against itself on the basis of the judgement it received from outside. But receiving external criticism means transforming it into self-criticism. If Christianity rejects the idea that it is a religion, it must fight in itself everything by which it becomes a religion. With some justification one can say that the two essential expressions of religion in the narrower sense are myth and cult. If Christianity fights against itself as a religion it must fight against myth and cult, and this it has done. It did so in the Bible, which, one should not forget, is not only a religious but also an antireligious book. The Bible fights for God against religion. This fight is rather strong in the Old Testament, where it is most powerful in the attack of the prophets against the cult and the polytheistic implications of the popular religion. In harsh criticism the whole Israelitic cult is rejected by some early prophets, and so is the mythology which gives the national gods ultimate validity. The God of Israel has been 'demythologized' into the God of the universe, and the gods of the nations are 'nothings'. The God of Israel rejects even Israel in the moment when she claims him as a national god. God denies his being *a* god.

The same fight against cult and myth is evident in the New Testament. The early records of the New Testament are full of stories in which Jesus violates ritual laws in order to exercise love, and in Paul the whole ritual law is dispossessed by the appearance of the Christ. John adds demythologization to deritualization: the eternal life is here and now, the divine judgement is identical with the acceptance or rejection of the light which shines for everybody. The early Church tried to demythologize the idea of God and the meaning of the Christ by concepts taken from the Platonic-Stoic tradition. In all periods theologians tried hard to show the transcendence of the divine over the finite symbols expressing him. The idea of 'God above God' (the phrase I used in *The Courage To Be*) can be found implicitly in all patristic theology. Their encounter with pagan polytheism, i.e. with gods on a finite basis, made the Church Fathers extremely sensitive to any concept which would present God as being analogous to the gods of those against whom they were fighting. Today this particular encounter, namely with polytheism, no longer has manifest reality; therefore the theologians have become careless in safeguarding their idea of a personal God from slipping into 'henotheistic' mythology (the belief in *one* god who, however, remains particular and bound to a particular group).

The early theologians were supported by the mystical element which in the fifth century became a powerful force in Christianity. The main concept of mysticism is immediacy: immediate participation in the divine Ground by elevation into unity with it, transcending all finite realities and all finite symbols of the divine, leaving the sacramental activities far below and sinking cult and myth into the experienced abyss of the Ultimate. Like the prophetical and the theological critique, this is an attack against religion for the sake of religion.

The ritual element was devaluated by the Reformation, in the theology of both the great reformers and of the evangelical radicals. One of the most cutting attacks of Luther was directed against the *vita religiosa*, the life of the *homini religiosi*, the monks. God is present in the secular realm; in this view Renaissance and Reformation agree. It was an important victory in the fight of God against religion.

The Enlightenment brought a radical elimination of myth and cult. What was left was a philosophical concept of God as the bearer of the moral imperative. Prayer was described by Kant as something of which a reasonable man is ashamed if surprised in it. Cult and myth disappear in the philosophy of the eighteenth century, and the Church is redefined by Kant as a society with moral purposes.

All this is an expression of the religious or quasi-religious fight against religion. But the forces which were fighting to preserve Christianity as a religion were ultimately stronger, in defence and counterattack. The main argument used in the counterattacks is the observation that the loss of cult and myth is the loss of the revelatory experience on which every religion is based. Such experience needs self-expression to continue, and that means it needs mythical and ritual elements. Actually they are never lacking. They are present in every religion and quasi-religion, even in their most secularized forms. An existential protest against myth and cult is possible only in the power of myth and cult. All attacks against them have a religious background, which they try to conceal, but without success. We know today what a secular myth is. We know what a secular cult is. The totalitarian movements have provided us with both. Their great strength was that they transformed ordinary concepts, events and persons into myths, and ordinary performances into rituals; therefore they had to be fought with other myths and rituals – religious and secular. You cannot escape them, however you demythologize and deritualize. They always return and you must always judge them again. In the fight of God against religion the fighter for God is in the paradoxical situation that he has to use religion in order to fight religion.

It is a testimony to present-day Christianity that it is aware of this situation. We have mentioned the opposition to the concept of religion in the philosophy of religion as one of the symptoms of this fight. We have used the word demythologize. We have used the term quasi-religion to indicate that man's ultimate concern can express itself in secular terms. We find contemporary theologians (like Bonhoeffer martyred by the Nazis) maintaining that Christianity must become secular, and that God is present in what we do as citizens, as creative artists, as friends, as lovers of nature, as workers in a profession, so that it may have eternal meaning. Christianity for these men has become an expression of the ultimate meaning in the actions of our daily life. And this is what it should be.

And now we have to ask: what is the consequence of this judgement of Christianity of itself for its dealing with the world religions? We have seen, first of all, that it is a mutual judging which opens the way for a fair valuation of the encountered religions and quasi-religions.

Such an attitude prevents contemporary Christianity from attempting to 'convert' in the traditional and depreciated sense of this word. Many Christians feel that it is a questionable thing, for instance, to try to convert Jews. They have lived and spoken with their Jewish friends for decades. They have not converted them, but they have created a community of conversation which has changed both sides of the dialogue. Some day this ought to happen also with people of Islamic faith. Most attempts to convert them have failed, but we may try to reach them on the basis of their growing insecurity in face of the secular world, and they may come to self-criticism in analogy to our own self-criticism.

Finally, in relation to Hinduism, Buddhism and Taoism, we should continue the dialogue which has already started and of which I tried to give an example in the third chapter: not conversion, but dialogue. It would be a tremendous step forward if Christianity were to accept this! It would mean that Christianity would judge itself when it judges the others in the present encounter of the world religions.

But it would do even more. It would give a new valuation to secularism. The attack of secularism on all present-day religions would not appear as something merely negative. If Christianity denies itself as a religion, the secular development could be understood in a new sense, namely as the indirect way which historical destiny takes to unite mankind religiously, and this would mean, if we include the quasi-religions, also politically. When we look at the formerly pagan, now Communist, peoples, we may venture the idea that the secularization of the main groups of present-day mankind may be the way to their religious transformation.

This leads to the last and most universal problem of our subject: does our analysis demand either a mixture of religions or the victory of one religion, or the end of the religious age altogether? We answer: none of these alternatives! A mixture of religions destroys in each of them the concreteness which gives it its dynamic power. The victory of *one* religion would impose a particular religious answer on all other particular answers. The end of the religious age – one has already spoken of the end of the Christian or the Protestant age – is an impossible concept. The religious principle cannot come to an end.

For the question of the ultimate meaning of life cannot be silenced as long as men are men. Religion cannot come to an end, and a particular religion will be lasting to the degree in which it negates itself as a religion. Thus Christianity will be a bearer of the religious answer as long as it breaks through its own particularity.

The way to achieve this is not to relinquish one's religious tradition for the sake of a universal concept which would be nothing but a concept. The way is to penetrate into the depth of one's own religion, in devotion, thought and action. In the depth of every living religion there is a point at which the religion itself loses its importance, and that to which it points breaks through its particularity, elevating it to spiritual freedom and with it to a vision of the spiritual presence in other expressions of the ultimate meaning of man's existence.

This is what Christianity must see in the present encounter of the world religions.

1. *Christianity and the Encounter of the World Religions*, The American Bampton Lectures, 1963, Columbia University Press.

7. THE UNKNOWN CHRIST OF HINDUISM

Raymond Panikkar

I was found by them that did not seek me. I appeared openly to them that asked not after me.

Romans 10:20; cf. Isaiah 65:1

1. THE SEARCH FOR A MEETING PLACE

On the encounter between East and West there is an almost overwhelming amount of literature. This fact alone proves that the problem is not merely a burning question, but also that it appears today in an altogether new perspective.

We do not intend to complicate this already complex problem; we should just like to sketch a very simple answer to the following question.

Where do Hinduism and Christianity meet? Or in other words, what is the *meeting place* for a fruitful dialogue between Hinduism and Christianity? Or again, if Christianity aims at being the universal religion, what is the starting point from which it can set out towards an encounter with Hinduism? Or, from a Hindu point of view, where and how can Hinduism face the challenge of the nature and presence of Christianity? We could put our question like this: where can a real encounter take place so that both having met, there could no longer be room any more for ignoring each other, but only room for a catholic embrace, an exclusive substitution or a mutual interpenetration? Strict segregation is neither desirable, nor possible any longer.

Even at the cost of unpleasant consequences we should no longer avoid putting the question directly. A simple co-existence, even if comfortable or desirable from a short-sighted, practical point of view, will not do. It will never satisfy the essential claim of Christianity to be the *Mystery* that God has revealed for the whole world,[1] and in consequence, it would be a source of internal (Christian) corruption, or a cause of external 'compensation' in the form of unexpected and unlawful attacks upon other creeds. Nothing is so harmful as what modern psychology would call 'unnatural suppression'. Either Christianity gives up its claim to universality, catholicity, and then peacefully co-exists with other religions, or it has to substantiate its claim by a theory – in the classical sense of the word – that shows the reasonableness and justness of its claims. Otherwise it would appear, as sometimes and for some people it has appeared, a fanatical and exclusive religion that aims at destroying everything that is not of its 'particular' taste.

Hinduism likewise cannot agree with mere co-existence. For either it co-exists with a militant Christianity thus endangering its own existence, or it co-exists with a mere passive Christianity which respects the present *status quo*. But this latter alternative based on a fundamental tenet of Hinduism – the relative equality of all religions – would mean the dissolution of Christianity as such and its conversion into one of the many Hindu branches. This amounts to saying that the Hindu claim for co-existence would mean a claim for the destruction of Christianity and what it stands for. Or, in other words, this claim for an innocent co-existence is much more radical than the Christian claim for conversion, for a theoretically co-existing Christianity would no longer be Christianity, whereas conversion does not mean destruction, but sublimation, transcendence, realization.

That is to say, Christianity devoid of its claim of being the universal religion (and in consequence of its having a right – or rather a duty and a responsibility before the whole world), would not be Christianity. Hinduism, on the other hand, without its belief in being the adequate and proper religion for Hindus, would no longer be Hinduism. There is apparently no place for both, if both have to be loyal to their essential nature.

The problem then arises in a manner so acute, that we have not the right to overlook it by proffering the excuse that an apparent and superficial cordiality is better left undisturbed. If we do not tackle the problem in all humility and sincerity, then we shall never overcome an underground uneasiness that will emerge only to grow destructive and harmful to both sides at critical moments in the history of individuals and of the two communities. Christianity desires that the Hindu become a Christian. Hinduism has no such wish to make Christians Hindus – to the Hindu one cannot in fact become what one is not; yet Hinduism will obviously prohibit Hindus from being unfaithful to their Hindu *dharma*. Is there any solution to this problem?

We here presuppose a deep human honesty in searching for the truth whenever it can be found, an intellectual openness in this search without bias or prejudice, and also a profound loyalty towards one's own religion. The religious quest of olden times, in which the peoples of the world either lived isolated or in subjection, was mainly directed towards the monodimensional deepening of one's own religion. The authentic religious urge of today can no longer overlook this thirst for an open dialogue and for mutual understanding. The religion of my brother becomes also for me a personal religious problem.

Moreover, religions themselves are craving for mutual help and enlightenment, not only externally because of the present unreligious wave, but also internally because of the dynamism, both intellectual and existential, which moves them towards an encounter. Intellectually, because no religion can boast to have deciphered fully the mystery of man and God; existentially, because man himself suffers more and more the attraction, as well as the repulsion, of other religions. The meeting of religions is an inmost religious problem. A missionary zeal without knowledge and love would have disastrous consequences. A proud isolation without care for others would be impious selfishness and cause the ruin of one's own religion.

A Christian who would undermine the foundation on which Hinduism rests, would not only be dishonest and un-Christian, but above all would be ineffective. A Hindu who would offer the due resistance to such an undermining would not only make any co-existence impossible or hypocritical, but would also be violating such fundamental tenets of Hinduism as tolerance and openness. The results of such a cold war would only be the growth of irreligion and atheism.

Our first dialectical step towards the answer is that a true encounter can only take place where the two 'things' really meet. Any encounter must be mutual. I cannot meet a cinema artist on the screen, primarily because, though I may somehow come to 'know' him, he does not meet me there. Christianity cannot meet Hinduism where Hinduism simply ignores Christianity; and vice versa, Hinduism will never meet Christianity where Christianity does not meet Hinduism. That is to say, the real meeting does not belong to the mere doctrinal level, because we are dealing here with two fully developed and independent religions. The comparative study of religion will not yield any lasting fruits unless the doctrines are merely considered as starting points for reaching the reality underlying them. It is not mainly a doctrinal affair but, as we said, a religious problem.

2. CHRIST, THE POINT OF ENCOUNTER

The true encounter between Christianity and Hinduism is only possible where they really *meet.* And they do not really meet in the doctrinal sphere, but in another deeper stratum that could well be called the existential level, or the 'ontic intentional' stratus.

The doctrines, despite their undeniable similarities, are far removed from each other and yet somehow have the same aim and point to the same goal. Moreover, they start from the same anthropological situation. In both cases, the same human being is found in his naked existence, striving to reach his fullness and perfection. Indeed, the Christian will say that Christian existence is already a supernatural gift, a 'new creation', a higher position. But he will not deny that the newness of 'grace' descends upon human existence as it is, and is somehow given to all human beings, since God wants the salvation of everyone and without 'grace' there is no salvation. Christianity will also say that its specific goal is already coloured by its own constituents, namely the divinization of man as Christianity understands it. That is to say, it claims to have a unique knowledge: a 'gnoseological intentionality', namely the gnosis that God is Trinity and our union is with God in Christ; but it will not contest the fact that the 'ontic intentionality' is the same, namely that very union with the Absolute.

The 'ontic intentionality' or goal of existence can

obviously not be properly expressed by mere words; for example we have used the expression, 'union with the Absolute', whereas a Yogin would prefer to say 'pure isolation' and a Buddhist, 'Nirvana'.

There is neither Absolute to be united with, nor duality to give the union any sense, they will say, and yet the 'ontic' goal intended is one and the same: it is precisely that end, that final stage, understood in one way or another, that all are aiming at. In other words, Christianity and Hinduism meet in a common endeavour, which has the same starting point and the same 'ontic' goal.

We should like now to develop this idea using a Christian terminology. In fact, it is not a bias in favour of Christianity if we choose the Christian standpoint. After all, it is Christianity that comes forward to meet Hinduism – Hinduism has been quite unconcerned until now, without caring for any meeting – and in consequence it falls to Christianity to clarify its position. And here is our simple statement, the explanation of which, however, may not be so simple: Christianity and Hinduism both meet in Christ. Christ is their meeting point. The real encounter can only take place in Christ, because only in Christ do they meet. We cannot 'prove' this statement rationally. We can only try to show, on the one hand, that they do not meet at any other point, and that on the other hand, according to Christianity and according to Hinduism as well, they can only meet in Christ, if they meet at all.

3. INSUFFICIENCY OF MERE DOCTRINAL PARALLELISMS

It is obvious that a real and living meeting or encounter cannot consist only in discovering certain similarities or common features in practical life and in the realm of ideas. Christianity and Hinduism are two living realities that cannot be confused with a set of ideas or a collection of practices. Even so, most of the existing common aspects are common only when they have been disconnected from the whole, and are mutually compared against an abstract and sterilized background which does not belong to either of them.

There is, for instance, a doctrine of grace in Christianity and there is also a similar doctrine in at least one of the important branches of Hinduism; but in spite of their similarities, which have sometimes been over-emphasized, and in spite of certain common aims towards which both tend, this doctrine offers only a meeting place for an academic and rather philosophical, or at least doctrinal, discussion between experts in the two theologies. Important as it may be, this or any other 'doctrine' will never be the ultimate basis for an integral encounter between Hinduism and Christianity.

We do not at all wish to minimize the importance of theoretical studies. Mutual knowledge is indispensable, but knowledge must be at the service of reality and must be led by a higher wisdom on which rests the whole integral issue. The integral question is not, for instance, whether the idea of 'grace' in Saivism is similar to the idea of 'grace' according to Christianity, but whether the good Saivite has all that he needs with his 'grace' and his religion and will not need to become a Christian, or vice-versa.

Hinduism and Christianity have many similar ideas, and aims. These are the starting points for dialogue and for a series of comparisons, but these belong to an intermediate stage which has to be dug down to its foundations and followed through to its consequences, if a real encounter is to take place.

The foundations of such a dialogue are, on the one hand, the *fundamental tenets* out of which the doctrines are developed, and, on the other hand, the reality, the *existential truth* which the doctrines try to explain. Both these dimensions transcend the doctrinal sphere. Either you have or you have not that particular conviction; either that reality, that aspect of the truth has been disclosed, revealed to you, or it has not. There is little to discuss, or even to think of on that level.

The consequences derived from comparative studies could be classified according to the following simple dialectical scheme: either the two 'theories' under comparison will be found equally right or they will not.

In the first case the identity can be absolute when we discover that both 'theories' are in fact the same, or simply relative when we come to the conclusion that both perform the same 'function' within a different doctrinal framework. They would then be merely equivalent. In both cases we shall have to proceed further, up to the point where the two religions differ, and then seek the 'reasons' for the difference. In spite of all theoretical equalities we shall reach the point of a historical 'otherness', for one religion is not in fact the other. Let us imagine for a moment that Sankara's Vedanta is theoretically equal to Thomas Aquinas's Scholasticism. In spite of such a theoretical parallelism the fact would still remain that one is still a *Hindu* doctrine and the other a *Christian* one. They would be the same intellectual garb for a different historical reality.

If the two theories being studied are not found equally right, the less accurate should disappear and make room for the other, or at least be corrected by the more accurate. But in fact experience proves to us not only that we shall hardly be able to convince our opponent, but also that he will not be able to give up his doctrine, because it is intimately welded to the core of his faith, which he holds because of supra-rational motives. Let us imagine a 'Thomist' constrained to accept that his proofs for the existence of God in fact do not prove their object. He will surely then have to give up those proofs, but he would not easily concede that God's existence is not 'provable'.

The real encounter in fact takes place at a much deeper level. 'Theories' belong only to an intermediate stage in between the existential foundation of a supra-rational faith and the ethical consequences of practical life.

4. INADEQUACY OF A MERELY CULTURAL SYNTHESIS

The deep encounter between Hinduism and Christianity cannot take place either on the profane or secular level of a merely cultural relationship. It is not about the meeting of two cultures that we speak, but of two religions. It is important to stress this point in our times, because there is a trend, a very well-intentioned but wrong tendency to reduce the encounter of religions to a problem of interrelation of cultures.

Indeed, Hinduism has produced a Hindu culture, and in spite of all our reserves, we cannot deny the existence of a certain Christian culture, nor the fact that the so-called Western culture is a product, or a by-product at least, of Christianity. But the laws of the interrelation of cultures are not the same as those of the meeting between religions. For the latter the allegiance to the past and the fidelity to oneself even at the cost of the renunciation of many other values, play an important part; for the former pragmatic criteria and purely cultural values are decisive.

In the problem of the relationship of cultures we shall have to ask first of all what is suitable for mankind, or for a certain country, in these times of growth in which no people or civilization can shut itself off from the rest of the world. How can progress and welfare be reached in the social structure of a country facing the problems of today? This is the cultural question. The religious question has a tremendous influence on such a cultural problem; but the guiding principles of the meeting of religions are of a different kind altogether. A true Hindu and a true Christian will not meet as two professors or two scholars, facing the problem of the interrelation of cultures – with a certain estrangement from their own cultures – and trying to find a synthesis or at least a syncretistic solution that would enable people to profit from an alien culture while retaining their indigenous values as much as possible. It is not a 'summit' meeting of 'great' politicians with full power to find by themselves a peaceful solution, but a humble encounter of living and loving persons trying to show fidelity to the higher and supreme Will of God – to put it in a personalistic way. Not shrewdness in the dealings, but obedience to God is their prime virtue. Culture is a manmade product. Religion owes an unshakeable fidelity to God. It is man-received and as such moulded and formed, but it is ultimately a God-given gift.

The meeting of religions must be carried out in a religious spirit considering ourselves instruments of God, being moved only by his grace that calls all men to him, dispelling all kinds of pettiness with regard to our own religious tradition and all prejudices regarding others and yet, at the same time, remaining faithful to our deep convictions, inspired only by the love for God and for our fellow beings, without desiring anything else than what God 'wants' us to do. The meeting of religions is not merely an intellectual endeavour, not a simple practical problem; it is in itself a religious experience and a religious task; it is the meeting of God in my friend who follows another path and perhaps even denies God or at least my conception of God – for though I cannot help having a conception of my own, the living God I worship is not an ideal of my mind, a concept, but transcends all understanding. Religions meet where religions take their source. Religions do not meet merely in ideas or in ideals. Religions meet in religion. For the present we cannot develop this point any further.[2]

This last idea will lead us to the second part of our statement.

5. THE EXISTENTIAL ENCOUNTER

We have tried so far to show that the true meeting of religions does not belong primarily to the essential, but to the existential sphere. Religions may meet in my heart, and not only in my ideas. By heart we do not mean any sentimental motive but the concrete reality of our lives. The encounter is the shock produced by two realities, but the meeting place is one. In my heart I can either embrace both religions in a personal synthesis (which may be intellectually more or less perfect and achieved), or destroy and replace one of the two which would have been 'killed' by my very love for it. It is here where religion exists, where religions may truly 'co-ek-sist' (it is then rather an 'in-esse' than a 'co-esse'). Meanwhile they can only sincerely *co-ek-sist*, by *co-in-sisting* (i.e. in dialogue).

A Christian will never 'under-stand' Hinduism if he is not con-verted to Hinduism. Never will a Hindu 'under-stand' Christianity unless he becomes a Christian. Which of the two religions is capable of sustaining such an embrace? We shall say a word about this later on.

Not everybody is bound to 'meet' everybody. There are very dangerous 'meetings'. Not everyone is even capable – and much less obliged – to *incarnate* himself in another religion and *redeem* the authentic core of the latter. But if an encounter has to be something more than a 'diplomatic' move, we cannot escape its exigencies. Moreover, since this encounter is not only an individualistic affair, but a collective, an *ecclesial* endeavour, the persons somehow involved in such an encounter will have to fulfil their part in this task, which belongs to the true dynamism of history.

Let us describe first the encounter from a general point of view in its existential and ultimate dimension.

There is Hinduism as a way of life, a path to mysticism, a religion leading the men of India towards their end; fulfilment and salvation. 'Leading' may be a misleading word; Hinduism hardly commands or leads. It is the Hindu who will find *moksa* if he lets himself be led, if he follows the Hindu *dharma.* Moreover fulfilment and salvation can be interpreted in completely different ways, some of which would not be recognized by Hinduism as such. There is Christianity also claiming to do the same, and also aspiring to have 'jurisdiction' over the men and women of the Hindu culture and religion. Both may agree or differ in several points, but the historical, concrete and almost juridical fact remains that on the one side stands Hinduism and on the other, Christianity. The born-Indian stands and is caught in between.

The encounter might become almost a clash. Here is Hinduism following a certain line and accepting a certain pattern of life, and then Christianity breaks in with the demand that the Hindu line be continued till it reaches

Christian fullness and the Hindu pattern 'con-verted' into the Christian one. The initiative comes from Christianity, and therefore the duty of justifying it belongs to it too. What does Christianity find in the Hindu that makes it also claim 'jurisdiction' over him? Does Christianity really want to destroy Hinduism and are all its activities 'tactics' if not 'tricks' to win Hindus over and so increase its numbers?

The history of that encounter cannot hide the fact that often the Hindu has received the impression that Christianity has been aiming just at pure recruitment of followers. We are not concerned now with a historical justification, explanation or excuse for these facts and their causes. The possible abuses of a certain right or the obvious dangers of any vital dynamism are beyond the scope of our reflections now. Regarding historical judgement I would just say: 'He who is free from sin may throw the first stone.'

Our problem is rather this: has Christianity in this encounter any justification at all for claiming a right over the Hindu or even over Hinduism itself? Christianity would rather speak of its duty in relation to the Hindu and Hinduism. Right or duty, it comes ultimately to the same. A rational proof of such a right or duty can hardly be given. Christianity is convinced that it has such an obligation, this conviction belongs to its faith and it would be almost the same thing to recognize this fact as to embrace Christianity. It belongs to the – occasionally tragic – tension of history that such an encounter is not a peaceful co-existence but a painful growth and development.

But it will at least clarify the positions to describe the exigencies of such an encounter in all sincerity and openness. Moreover, Christianity can also perhaps show that its claim, be it true or not, is not an unjust and evil one, but a logical and honest consequence of its nature, and even a good and desirable one, once its tenets are understood. Here they stand, Hinduism and Christianity meeting together not in agreement, but in tension, and perhaps opposition, on this ultimate level of two living and existing religions.

Before proceeding further we should now try to characterize this ultimate ground of that encounter between Hinduism and Christianity according first to Hinduism and secondly to Christianity.

6. THE HINDU GROUND OF THE ENCOUNTER

Hinduism is such an exuberant and rich religion that it does not have to fear Christianity. Moreover, it believes that it has room even for Christianity inside its own manifold structure. At least so Hinduism believes, though undoubtedly the Hindu idea of Christianity does not coincide with the consciousness Christianity has of itself. That is the reason why Hinduism thinks itself to be tolerant, though Christianity is afraid that this seeming tolerance is the highest form of intolerance: only to allow to others the place it has allotted to them.

Hinduism has not always taken the attitude we are going to describe, but we think it is a typical Hindu feature and undoubtedly one of modern Hinduism. Hinduism welcomes Christianity as *another* religion, and is glad to receive it as a younger sister religion, and might be inclined to accept and even to integrate with Christianity if only Christianity would give up its claim of exclusiveness and, in consequence, its pretension of being ultimate. Hinduism believes that all religions are good in so far as they lead men towards perfection. It would claim a certain superiority, as that of an elder sister, regarding theological doctrines and mystical insights, but this would be only secondary. What it defends against Christianity is its right to be the religion of the Hindus; and, even if much pressed, it could agree that the way of one born in India might be the Christian way, it would, however, by all means defend the right of its own existence, since ultimately it believes that it is the most perfect expression of the *sanatana dharma* – of the everlasting religion, at least in its higher form.

They meet as older and younger sisters; they meet as *two* religions, two ways which eventually may even need mutual correction and mutual enlightenment, but which must always remain distinct. Hinduism finds it scandalous and almost incomprehensible that other religions are not able to accept this standpoint, and that they refuse the sincere and democratic collaboration that Hinduism offers them.

Hinduism somehow projects its caste mentality into the encounter with other religions. Each religion is like a separate caste (which in Hinduism does not mean anything abhorrent) within which an individual reaches his goal by performing his duty and following his own *dharma*. No matter what our 'caste', we all meet in the common end through the parallel fulfilment of our duties.

A recent form of Hinduism however, harassed by the needs of modern times, is inclined to indulge in a peculiar syncretism which remains nevertheless very Hindu. It would be ready, so to speak, to sacrifice itself as a particular religion, provided the other religions would do the same, and be transformed in a universal – 'catholic' – religion without limitations of any kind, of cult, dogmas and the like. We should then meet in the pure nakedness of a religion without contents, in an *élan*, an aspiration of man towards perfection, fullness, and bliss. According to this Neo-Hinduism, we should renounce everything that separates, that hurts us, that curtails our freedom and the expansion of our being.

For a long time Hinduism, which through the multiplicity of its religious forms has suffered and experienced at least like any other religion the imperfections of the human mind and the limitations of the heart, has dreamed of this universal and boundless religion. We only meet in the Absolute; we only meet at the end of our pilgrimage; we encounter one another once we realize that we are one and the same reality. We cannot meet in our differences; we shall only meet in what unites us. We should give up what makes us different and renounce all our ideas, conceptions and practices. Truth, Silence, Love – these would be the only dogmas of this new religion in which all men would meet.

In summary this would be the position of Hinduism: either we meet as sister-religions striving towards the same end, or we meet by sacrificing our individual ways in the mysterious, divine, basis of our Origin and End.

7. THE CHRISTIAN GROUND OF THE ENCOUNTER

Christianity would be willing to accept that challenge of Hinduism and we hope to show that Hinduism and Christianity meet precisely in the framework proposed by the former. Let us first expound the Christian position and, secondly, the Christian answer to the Hindu point of view. We have already proposed the Christian answer: we all meet in Christ, because he is the ontological meeting point of any religion as well as of any positive ultimate value. We might perhaps explain the Christian standpoint like this: Hinduism and Christianity as two God-believing religions undoubtedly meet in God. We do not say that they meet in their conception of God, but in God, in the Absolute, in the Ultimate. And now comes the Christian elaboration of this meeting ground, which does not seek to win the acquiescence of the Hindu, but only his understanding of it.

We all meet in God. God is not only everywhere but everything is in him, and we, including all our strivings and actions, are *of* him, *in* him, *from* him, *to* him. (One could equally well have said 'It' in this context.) Now, there is only one link, one mediator between God and the rest. That is Christ, from whom everything has come, in whom everything subsists, to whom everything that shall endure the bite of time will come. It is Christ who leads every man to God; there is no other way but through him. It is Christ who inspires the prayers of man and 'hears' them. It is he who whispers to us any divine inspiration and who speaks as God, whatever forms the 'patient' of the divine may believe in or think of. He is the Light that illumines every human being coming into this world.

Hence, for Christianity, Christ is already there in Hinduism in so far as Hinduism is a true religion; Christ is already at work in any Hindu prayer as far as it is really prayer; Christ is behind any form of worship, in as much as it is adoration made to God. Christianity will not judge Hinduism; only God in Christ will judge. Christianity will not and has not the right to sift and sever the wheat from the chaff, so long as men are pilgrims on earth. It will take and meet Hinduism as it is and will find Christ there because he is already there, as he is also with the poor and the thirsty and the prisoner and the persecuted.

A very important point now arises, and this is the specific

character of Christianity: the historical and concrete dimension of Christ which is yet 'inseparable' and 'indivisible' from his divinity and his cosmic action.

That Christ which is already in Hinduism, which, therefore, Christianity recognizes and worships, that Christ has not unveiled his whole face, has not yet completed his mission there. He still has to grow up and to be recognized. Moreover, he still has to be crucified there, dying with Hinduism as he died with Judaism and with the Hellenistic religions in order to rise again, as the same Christ (who is already in Hinduism), but then as a risen Hinduism, as Christianity. The case of Judaism presents a unique historical feature indeed, but the analogy still holds.

We meet in Christ; Christ is there in Hinduism, but Hinduism is not yet his spouse. Hinduism is the desired bride whose betrothal was celebrated long ago in the Vedic times, and whose marriage still remains in the mystery of history. Christ appears there to the eyes of the Christians, somewhat as a prisoner in a body which still has to die and to rise again, to be converted into 'Church' in the precise theological sense of the word.

This explains the paradoxical attitude of Christianity: it loves Hinduism and meets Hinduism not perhaps as a sister, but as a mother – Christianity being the religion of the *last* times, of the *new* Covenant – as a mother however that has to leave her old body and transmit all her vitality and virtues to her own child, to the child she begets because it is the same life that is being breathed in both places; and yet it is a 'new' creature. Christianity loves Hinduism because it discovers Christ in it, but this same love kills Hinduism as being a separated body and accepts it as a risen-Christian body. Only the Christian belief in the tremendous mystery of death and resurrection can justify the Christian position. He himself, the Christian, is born a 'pagan' and must first be converted – he must die and rise again in order to become a son of God, a partaker of the divine life. He does not want for Hinduism anything more than what he wants for himself.

Conversion does not mean, speaking from a Christian point of view, a changing 'over' to another culture, another tradition or even 'another' religion, but a changing 'in', a changing into a new life, a new existence, a new creation, which is precisely the old one – and not another – but transformed, lifted up, risen again.

If we were not afraid of paradoxes, we would say that Hinduism and Christianity meet in the depths of death, in the denial of ourselves and the acceptance of divine life deposited germinally at the moment of our rebirth or rather, still deeper, at the moment of the death – and resurrection – of Christ in the cross. 'If the grain of wheat does not die . . .'

8. CHRIST, THE MEETING PLACE

The presence of Christ in Hinduism makes it, in the eyes of Christian theology, not *another* religion altogether, but a vestibule of Christianity, a first and valuable stage of the *sanatana dharma* which has to find its fullness in the truly *sanatana* but *dharma-siddhi* of Christianity (the *dharma-sadhana* of Hinduism being Christianity).

Hinduism has no dogmas, Hinduism has no essential contents. Being only the concrete expression of the existential *dharma*, Hinduism can take as many forms as the circumstances require, each of them being relative to time and space. Christianity's bold claim is that it provides the true contents, for the time being, that is, during this earthly pilgrimage (in 'heaven' there are no sacraments, no dogmas because faith has fulfilled its mission) to the Hindu existential *dharma.* Its claim can only be substantiated by Christian faith itself which believes that God, who has 'spoken' through the prophets and *rishis* (sages), has finally sent his living and personal word – one with him – to fulfil all justice, all *dharmas.*

In this sense Christian dogma, Catholic faith – both in the precise theological sense – meet the challenge of universality that the modern Hindu mind finds absolutely necessary. That new claim of the Hindu *dharma* is not strictly speaking a kind of syncretism – though it often takes this form – but it is the voice of catholicity, it is the very dynamism of the existential *dharma* towards a sublimation of its own 'beliefs', tending to overcome all particularisms. When Christianity says that God is Christ, that Bliss is Heaven, that Perfection is Union with God, that Truth is the Logos, and so on, Christianity does not want to put limitations on those notions, but endeavours to fill them up with living contents, with a real meaning, in order to prevent them from degenerating into mere words, into vague and abstract aspirations that each individual would afterwards interpret in his own peculiar and restricted way. Christianity welcomes the 'sacrifice' that modern Hinduism demands from every particular religion in order to be *converted* into *the* Religion of mankind. Is it not a Christian injunction to hate one's soul, to deny oneself, to die fully in order to rise again into divine life and existence? Is not the mystery of the Cross the central core of Christianity? The only thing that it says is that universality, catholicity, openness and perfection do not mean vagueness, unbelief, purely abstract intention, nihilism and uprootedness from this earth and our human surroundings, so long as we still dwell here in this world. A Christian dogma is neither an idol, nor a limitation nor a definition of faith, nor a place in which to get stuck before attaining the goal. It is just the expression of the proper channel through which we reach the Absolute, it is just the way – not the end – we have to run along in order to reach the fullness.

The Catholic meaning of a dogma is not a 'truth' or a 'formula' that has to be believed in – Christian faith only believes in God, who is Father and Christ and Holy Spirit, unfolding more and more the mystery of God in concrete aspects – but a means to bridle our intellect in order that our higher knowledge may reach, as far as it is here possible, the unfathomable inner nature of the supreme. This should not in any way be taken as a subjective interpretation of the Christian truths or a relativization of the dogmas in a modernistic sense. Dogmas are necessary so long as we are intelligent beings, but we should beware of the danger of 'dogmatolatry'.

The jurisdiction Christianity seeks to wield over Hinduism, the right it claims over Hinduism, is not therefore a kind of juridical ownership. Christ does not belong to Christianity, he only belongs to God. It is Christianity and Hinduism as well, that belong to Christ, though in two different levels. Simply because Christ is fully present in the eucharist and the eucharist has been entrusted to the Church, Hinduism also has a right to have it, which comes to mean that Christianity has not the right to keep it for itself, but must offer it even to the Hindu. We have here another instance of the inversion or subversion of all human, created values after God's revelation in Christ!

The encounter of Melchizedech with Abraham, and later on the revelation of Peter at Joppa and the many experiences of Paul, are some of the authoritative instances of this Christian attitude and position, besides, of course, the living example of Christ and his explicit teachings,

Let us explain again the Christian position accepting now, without the distinctions that would be required, that main tenet of the equality of religions.

Hinduism seems to say: because we are all the same, we keep separate; because we are already one let us simply co-exist and not strive for a deeper unity for we are already the same ocean, our only difference being that you are one stream and we another; because monism is there, let us not pay attention to our present dualism which is only apparent.

Christianity would like to answer: because we are all the same – though not yet fully as experience proves it – let us discard this veil of *maya*, which is of an enormous historical thickness, let us embrace one another and not keep aloof any longer, but merge into the oneness we all desire, let us *discover* this unity, let us mix our waters and realize that identity you are convinced of and which we are striving for. If there are still some differences they will disappear like the liquid level of two vessels once they are connected. He who has more will spontaneously give if the other does not refuse the gift. The encounter of the two rivers may produce some passing waves or some sudden whirlpools, but the enrichment will be mutual. Christianity's claim of catholicity has as a logical counterpart the fact that Christianity is not complete Christianity – i.e. catholic – so long as that unity has not been realized. We are not self-sufficient monads, but fragments of the same, unique religion, though the level of the waters may be, and is, different; we need one another, because being one we are destined to become one. The Christian Church – Christianity – has the consciousness of being a very specially qualified 'fragment' indeed: the fulfilment of religion (the trunk in a certain sense). This is not, however, because of its actual per-*fection*, but because Christ, the Head of the Mystical Body, is really and sacramentally present in it, and its soul is the Holy Spirit. 'That all may be one' is precisely what drives Christianity to realize this oneness, which of course does not mean uniformity. Because as you say we *are* the same, let us really *be* the same! Christianity does not want assimilation, dominion, does not want to destroy; it only shares in the same wish of Hinduism: to be one!

I would dare to say even more. This thirst for unity, this prayer for oneness is so fundamental in Christianity that it conditions everything else. Obviously unity which is not based on truth is not unity at all, a oneness which is not the real one – willed by God, the Christian would say – is no oneness at all. This amounts to saying that no human compromise is a way towards union, that this union is not the result of sitting together and framing a liberal religious constitution, but of praying and also struggling together to dis-cover the Will of God, to realize this unity. But this amounts to saying also that though Christians are convinced of their beliefs, they do not know the further developments of their Church, they do not have access to the plans of divine providence, they do not cling to a fixed scheme or to a frozen faith. New dogmas, renewed formulation of old ones, homogeneous evolution and progress are constant features of Christianity. Nobody knows how Christianity will look when the present Christian waters and the Hindu river merge into a bigger stream, where the peoples of the future will quench their thirst – for truth, for goodness, for salvation.

There is little sense in discussing now in this context what Christianity considers definitive and what changeable. There is and there will be an identity and a continuity but it is not for the theologian to pontificate; it is not even for the pontiff to silence the prophet or to rule over the future. You follow me, said Christ to the first head of his Church, and do not bother about John. Sufficient for the day is the evil thereof!

Finally, a word about Christ himself for the Hindu. It looks really ridiculous, not to say preposterous from a Hindu point of view, to say that the encounter takes place in Christ. No Hindu would dare say that the meeting should take place in Vishnu for instance.

We are not concerned here in proving anything or in making any kind of apologetics, nor in dispelling the many misconceptions about Christ, given to the Hindus perhaps by Christians themselves. These are three very important points, but outside our scope. We are only making an attempt to clarify the issue.

The first thing to say regarding the place of Christ in contrast to any Hindu symbol of the divinity is that the statement we made about Christ makes sense at least for the Christian and can be made understandable – if not acceptable – to the Hindu too, whereas a parallel statement about Vishnu would not make sense for either of them.

Hinduism and Christianity will agree to some extent that both meet in God and that God is working inside both religions as it were. The Christian claim is that God and Christ are indivisible and inseparable, though yet without mixture and fusion, and that where God is at work in this world, as it were, it is always in and through Christ that he acts. Hinduism would not find much difficulty in accepting this and would call it perhaps Isvara (Lord). The stumbling-block appears when Christianity further identifies, with the required qualifications, Christ with Jesus the Son of Mary. A full Christian faith is required to accept this identity. The Hindu can only respect this belief which to him seems absurd. The way to the living Christ is not precisely pure reasoning.

9. THE CHRISTIAN ENCOUNTER

We must not linger any longer on this subject lest we be obliged to make a complete study of its implications and consequences. We wish however to add some few reflections of a more pastoral character.

The Christian encounter, we have already said, is not merely a doctrinal dialogue, nor a cultural mutual understanding. It is a historical encounter of religions, in the concrete meeting of men in society. This encounter can really and truly take place because it is an encounter in Christ already present in the heart of the two *bona fide* partners.

Mutual understanding is very necessary and it is an ineluctable condition. But knowledge alone will not do. Knowledge alone not only lacks the necessary warmth for an integral encounter, but has also an almost antagonistic effect. In fact, human knowledge is always an egocentric movement. The known 'thing' (doctrine, person) comes to me. I am at home and the host: I receive, welcome and assimilate the 'things' that I know, that is, I possess, I enrich myself.

Only mutual love overcomes that egocentric position of knowledge. When I love, I go out, I give up, I am the guest, I am no more at home, I am received and possessed. Pure knowledge hurts the rest of the non-*assimilated* things. I may reach some synthesis by an intellectual victory over my opponent. I bring only the spoils of the adversary to my system. Sankara, let us say, is overcome or understood, but the Sankarites remain outside, unconvinced.

The Christian encounter cannot be an intellectual victory; it is not in the triumph of 'Thomism' that the meeting can take place for instance. Not even in a confrontation of 'theologies' in the rather technical sense of the word, can the Christian encounter be realized. Only in Christ are the meeting and the embrace possible.

This requires from both sides, but especially from the Christian side, an asceticism, a mystical life, a detachment from all categories and formulae, not only from prejudices, but also 'judices', judgements too. This should not be taken as a denial of 'orthodoxy' but its integration into 'orthopraxy' (right action).

The real Christian encounter with other religions requires a very special asceticism, the stripping off of all external garbs and forms to remain alone with Christ, with the naked Christ, dead and alive on the Cross, dead and alive within the Christian too who dares such an encounter with his non-Christian brother. That special kind of asceticism means real mysticism, that is, the immediate contact with Christ which carries him beyond – not against – formulae and explanations. Only then is it possible to discover Christ there where he is now veiled with less correct or even wrong formulations, and help to unveil, to reveal the mystery hidden from the aeons in God. Only a few, unless a way is found, are capable of such a stripping off, and able to remain with the purely naked Christ living in them, performing this existential imitation of the incarnation of Christ.

The consequences reach very far and through them, in a way, the merely comparative *study* of religions, is doomed to failure. The study has to be done, but has also to be transcended. The meeting of spiritualities can only take place in the Spirit. No new 'system' has primarily to come out of this encounter, but a new and yet old *spirit* must emerge. Spiritualities are not there to be 'studied' – they cannot be properly 'studied' – but to be lived, or, we could add, to be experienced, if the word is kept free from any idea of artificial 'experimentation'. I repeat that the meeting of religions is a *religious* act – an act of incarnation and redemption.

It is an encounter in *naked Faith*, in *pure Hope*, in *supernatural Love* – and not a conflict of formulae, an expectation of getting them 'over' (where to?).

In naked *Faith*! I believe, *credo*! But not reifying living expressions of a mystical, because supernatural, act into a belief in crystallized and disconnected sentences. The act of faith is a gift of God by which I partake in the divine knowledge God has of himself and in himself of everything else; it is a vital simple act which needs only the minimum of intellectual explicitness. I believe (O Lord!) and this act alone is a saving one. I believe – in the only thing which requires this higher and supreme act, namely in the Absolute, in God. I realize him, still vaguely with no clear vision, yet I am fully convinced of him and somehow taste him already: in God, so my faith unfolds it, who is Trinity – Father, Logos and Holy Spirit. And again faith will let me into the unfathomable womb of the divinity and make me discover, realize, that this father is all-powerful, creator . . . and the Logos became man . . . and the Spirit breathes in his Church . . . But all these 'articles' of Faith are only expressions, manifestations, explicit examples of the mystical act of Faith, which has no full stops, no adequate intellectual expression, which can only be imperfectly translated into human words. In that Faith of the Christian, he, because it is Christ who inspires him, and is behind him, encounters his Hindu brother . . .

In pure *Hope*, in the supernatural consciousness of being already possessed by God, of being God's possession so as one day to break up in its fullness, in the pure expectation of God's manifestation and glory, the Christian is almost one with, or at least he embraces and includes already, his Hindu fellow men. He, in Hope, is already in possession – because he is possessed – of the new heaven and the new earth; he excludes no atom of being that is going to rise again; how could he exclude those men and women who may not 'believe' in the *Name* of Christ, but who are already pervaded by the same hope of liberation and union?

In supernatural *Love* the encounter is not only implicit, but explicit. The Christian does not only share the same hope, or embrace others in his faith, he actually meets Christ and communicates with him in the person of his brethren, the men on earth, without distinction of race, creed or condition. If he really loves, he discovers Christ already there. It is Christ himself who has awakened that love, and the Christian himself will not be able to explain how he came to possess it and be inflamed by it. Love unifies and makes one.

The Christian encounter is really much more than the meeting of two friends, it is the communion in being, in one Being which is much more intimate to both of them, than they themselves are; it is the communion not only in Christ, but of Christ. Nothing of condescension, nothing of paternalism or of superiority is to be found in the supernatural love of a Christian encounter. Neither teaching nor learning matters very much in the unity of love. He who has a higher temperature or a richer knowledge will spontaneously contaminate as it were, will automatically share his lot with the other, his neighbour.

Only when a man is completely empty of himself will Christ fully dwell in him. Only when he is totally stripped of himself, only when he is in the state of *kenosis*, of denial and annihilation, will Christ fulfil his incarnation in him. Only *kenosis* allows incarnation; and incarnation is the only factual way for redemption . . .

1. Cf Matthew 13:35; Romans 16:25f.; Ephesians 3:8; Colossians 1:26; etc.
2. May I perhaps recall an anecdote? I once attended a religious meeting in which a dialogue of a rather syncretistic bias was maintained with an indulgent harmonizing approach. Everyone disagreed through 'tolerance' and 'comprehension'; *tot capita quot sententiae!* Agreeing in the rather vague and 'liberal' framework, everybody had his own personal opinion. Only a Catholic priest and a Buddhist bikkhu, holding maximalist attitudes, found themselves in real agreement and were the only two united voices in that gathering.

8. DIALOGUE AS A CONTINUING CHRISTIAN CONCERN

Stanley Samartha

Dialogue is part of the living relationship between people of different faiths and ideologies as they share in the life of the community. Christians in different countries of the world are already engaged in dialogue with their neighbours. Factors in contemporary historic situations in which Christians find themselves today, and the theological imperatives of the Christian faith itself, make it necessary that this concern for dialogue be continued. Therefore, one of the essential tasks before us now is to acknowledge this fact, consider its possibilities and problems, and draw out its implications for the life and witness of the Church in a pluralistic world. What is the extent of our involvement in such encounters? What is the theological demand of the Christian faith that makes it part of our Christian obedience as we live with men of other faiths? What are the inner resources that sustain us, the criteria which judge our efforts and the limitations beyond which dialogue ceases to be faithful dialogue? These are a few questions to which some attention should be given here.

I

The Christian interest in other religions is, of course, not new. The early Church seriously grappled with issues raised by its encounters with the religions, philosophies and cultures of the Graeco-Roman world. In recent history the well-known Missionary Conferences – Edinburgh 1910, Jerusalem 1928 and Tambaram 1938 – took serious note of other religions.[1] The New Delhi Assembly, 1961, referred to 'Dialogue as a form of evangelism which is often effective today'.[2] Uppsala 1968 pointed out that 'the meeting with men of other faiths or of no faith must lead to dialogue. A Christian's dialogue with another implies neither a denial of the uniqueness of Christ, nor any loss of his own commitment to Christ, but rather that a genuinely Christian approach to others must be human, personal, relevant and humble'.[3] We must also recognize the Declaration of Vatican II on 'the Relationship of the Church to non-Christian Religions'.[4]

With regard to more recent meetings, at least three points may be made. First, there is an increasing participation by our Roman Catholic brethren. Whether at Kandy 1967, or Ajaltoun 1970, or Zürich 1970, Roman Catholics were present not just as observers, but as active participants, bringing in their scholarship, experience and insights from different parts of the world. There are, of course, underlying differences of theological approach, but the fact that Roman Catholics, Orthodox and Protestants could, together as Christians, meet men of other faiths is itself important. Second, in contrast to some of the earlier debates which moved almost exclusively in Western structures of thought and procedure, not always sensitive to or illumined by insights of Christians from other situations, in recent years, people from other parts of the world, particularly from Asia and Africa, with different cultural heritages and with actual experience of dialogues, have made stronger and more persistent contributions. In the period of world missionary conferences, their contributions were more or less interesting footnotes to what was largely a Western debate about other religions. Today, they are chapters in the growing ecumenical book. The point that is made here is not that dialogues are more important in Asia or Africa than in the West, but that the issues raised by dialogue are not limited to particular cultural contexts, but have larger ecumenical dimensions. Third, a fact of perhaps even greater significance is the actual participation by men of other faiths in dialogues initiated by Christians. It is no more just talk *about* dialogue by Christians among themselves, but the Christian involvement in dialogue *with* them, discussion of issues in their presence and with their active participation. This does not, of course, preclude theological reflection by Christians themselves, but it is more informed by the experience of actual dialogue. It is against this background that I now give a few examples of dialogues that have taken place in recent years. They are part of the historic context in which theological reflection on dialogue should take place.[5]

On 14–16 June 1962 a group of Hindu and Christian friends met in a Christian ashram near Kottayam, South India. Twenty-two people, fifteen Christians and seven Hindus, took part in the meeting. The theme was one of the most fundamental issues between Hindus and Christians touching their life and thought at the deepest level, viz. the Nature of Truth. It was considered under three sub-headings: the nature of Truth, the knowledge of Ultimate Truth and the relation of Ultimate Truth to Life in the world. It was one of the earliest occasions in India when our Roman Catholic friends joined the Orthodox and Protestants in such a venture.

Each day two half-hour periods, one in the morning and one in the evening, were set aside, which participants observed together as a period of silent prayer and meditation.

It is noted that 'the Hindu and Christian groups came to grips with the fundamental issues in the conversations and sought together to clarify the points of vital difference between *advaitic* (a particular school of Indian philosophy) and Christian understandings of Ultimate Truth, and explored the meaning of a community of concern and discourse in which dialogues on religious truths and on religious dimensions of cultural and social life could be fruitfully continued'. M. M. Thomas, who took part in this dialogue, wrote, 'Building a community of discourse with our Hindu brethren is essential if any communication is to take place between Christians and Hindus.'[6]

In 1968, on 27 and 28 January, at the end of the week of prayer for Christian Unity, a group of Roman Catholic, Orthodox and Protestant Christians met together with a group of Muslims at Selly Oak College, Birmingham, UK. It is significant that such a meeting was possible in Birmingham where people of different religious communities are living together and where, as a result, several problems have come up very sharply in recent years. A few quotations from the report are given here. With the long and violent history of Christian-Muslim relations in Europe and with the memories of the Crusades not forgotten, the group felt it necessary to say, 'We must never deal with each other simply as stereotyped or pigeon-holed representatives of another tradition. We must seek to know each other and respect each other as individuals . . . We should be less conscious of our different labels as "Christians" and "Muslims", than of our faithfulness to the one God . . . There might be paradox and even tension in our mutual understanding, but it could be constructive tension . . .' In the context of their day-to-day living in a multi-religious society with all its problems and tensions, two points emerged from the dialogue – the emphasis on certain beliefs common to the Christian and the Muslim and the need, expressed with a sense of urgency, to continue friendly relations. The report goes on to say, 'There was great need for continuing discussion and increasing society's awareness of the relevance of our common assumptions as Muslims and Christians. The supremacy of God, the availability of His revealed guidance, the expectation of an afterlife, the definition of right and wrong, of truth and falsehood, the sanctity of family life and all life – such are the issues we must maintain in an increasingly agnostic world. We look forward to further contacts and to working for and praying for a deeper reconciliation of Muslims and Christians in our service to men and to God, in our dialogue with each other and with God.'

Several dialogues between Christians and Jews have taken place in recent years. These conversations have not been easy. This is mainly because of historical reasons derived from the history of the Church in the West, partly because of theological differences, and now mostly because of political factors. On 27–30 October 1970, a meeting convened by the International Jewish Committee on Interreligious Consultations and the World Council of Churches was held in Lugano, Switzerland. The thirty participants came from England, France, Germany, Holland, India, Israel, Switzerland and the United States of America. The theme of the meeting, mutually agreed to, was 'The Quest for World Community – Jewish and Christian Perspectives'. Questions touching particularity and pluralism and the relationship between religion, peoplehood, nation-state and land were discussed from different points of view in an atmosphere of friendliness and openness, though not free from tensions generated by strongly divergent views. The fact that Christians and Jews could read together some of the Psalms at the beginning of each day emphasized the common roots of our spiritual heritage which, however, needs to be cultivated afresh with new tools and a larger vision of mankind in the Bible, which includes not only Abraham, Isaac and Jacob, but also Adam and Noah.

These examples have been of bilateral conversations between Christians and people of one other faith. But there have also been meetings in which people of several different faiths came together. On 8–9 October 1965 some thirty representatives from six major religions in Korea – Buddhism, Won-Buddhism, Confucianism, Chondoism, Catholicism and Protestantism – gathered together for a two-day session to consider the common tasks before them. The emphasis was not on the 'spirituality' of particular religions, but on what men of different religious persuasions could contribute to the solution of the pressing problems of the country. The religions were strongly criticized for their reluctance to be open, and were asked to co-operate with each other in practical tasks. The different religions, it was pointed out, claim to have a message, 'and believe that they are called to a mission to save the rest of the world, though they are not yet ready to join the new world which calls us to have open dialogue with our neighbours . . . This world is our common denominator upon which we are able to communicate with each other. And for us, in Korea, it is this troublesome nation with all its problems that is our field, where we can find the common task for all Korean religions.'

Invitations come with increasing frequency to the World Council of Churches to take part in world conferences on religion, some of which deal with specific issues. Such a World Conference on Religion and Peace met in Kyoto, Japan, this year (1970) from 16–22 October. It was attended by 285 persons belonging to ten major religions and coming from thirty-six countries. 'Blue-turbaned Sikh, Orthodox priest with flowing robe and hood, fez-wearing Muslim, shaven-headed Buddhist monk, business-suited rabbi, clergy-collared Protestant, crucifix-adorned Catholic Archbishop, orange-robed Hindu swami – they were all there' (*Japan Christian News*, No. 376, 30 October 1970). A Roman Catholic Archbishop from India was the chairman of the Conference, and among the considerable number of Christians present there were four members of the World Council staff and several who belong to its constituent churches and highest committees. Lest it be misunderstood that this Conference was just another 'parliament of religions' where the patience of the participants is tested by the number and length of the speeches, it must immediately be pointed out that the main focus was on the practical possibilities of peace, a theme that was discussed in relation to three specific areas, viz. human rights, disarmament and development. The Conference message said that they had all come together 'in peace out of a common concern for peace'. (Report: World Conference on Religion and Peace, WCRP/Doc. -030, Kyoto, Japan, 22 October 1970.)

The Ajaltoun Consultation on the theme 'Dialogue between Men of Living Faiths', held 16–25 March 1970, was authorized by the Central Committee at its meeting in Canterbury in August 1969. It took the form of a conversation between Hindus, Buddhists, Christians and Muslims regarding recent experiences and future possibilities of dialogue. The forty participants came from seventeen different countries. The following are some excerpts from the Ajaltoun Memorandum. 'The particular object of the Consultation was to gather the experiences of bilateral conversations between Christians and men of the major faiths of Asia with the full participation of members of these faiths, to experiment with a multilateral meeting and to see what could be learned for future relations between people of living faiths . . . It was the experience of the Consultation that something very new had been embarked upon. It was noted that this was the first time that men of these four faiths had been brought together under the auspices of the World Council of Churches . . . what was experienced together was felt to be very positive, a matter of general thankfulness and something to be carried forward urgently.'

'The keynote of the Consultation was the understanding that a full and loyal commitment to one's own faith did not stand in the way of dialogue. On the contrary, it was our faith which was the very basis of, and driving force to, intensification of dialogue and a search for common action between members of various faiths . . .'[7]

(Since this address was delivered to the Central Committee of the World Council of Churches in 1971, the World Council has sponsored several major bilateral and multilateral meetings between Christians and their neighbours of other faiths: Jews, Muslims, Hindus and Buddhists. A multilateral meeting in 1974, Colombo, brought together people of five religions: Hindus, Buddhists, Jews, Christians and Muslims. In addition, consultations have been held on African Traditional Religions, 1973 and 1978, and on Faith and Ideologies, 1975. The most important development since 1971 is the preparation of a set of *Guidelines* on Dialogue with People of Living Faiths and Ideologies adopted by the Central Committee at Kingston, Jamaica, in January 1979. Copies of all publications, including *Guidelines*, are available from the Publication Office, World Council of Churches, Geneva, Switzerland.)

II

These are a few selected examples of dialogues which have recently taken place in different parts of the world that provide us with the historic context in which we find ourselves today. Two brief observations must be made, however, to put them in a wider perspective. First there is the question of ideologies, particularly of Marxism. There has also been a series of dialogues between Christians and Marxists. It is important to note, however, that ideologies like Marxism cut across the boundaries of traditional religions, challenging their assumptions, questioning their structures and demanding that they be more concerned with this world and human life. It would be unwise to form 'a religious alliance' against ideologies in order to save and to perpetuate traditional religious institutions. But the questions raised by Marxism must be faced within the context of communities where people of different faiths and ideologies seek to live together and look for resources to build their common life.

Second, the impression should not be given that all dialogues are intellectual discourses or 'talking' about religious matters. There have also been meetings where no papers were read, where tired vocal chords were exercised to the minimum and where serious efforts were made to break through the structures of language, concepts and debate. Even within 'structured' dialogues, people tried to open themselves up to the symbols of religious life and practice, particularly to music and art, to devotion, meditation and the controlled use of silence. But one should recognize that verbal communication is also an essential part of dialogue for sharing in theological ideas, religious experience and practical concerns, without which it is difficult to build up a community of discourse and common involvement.

In all this, the fact that Christians – Roman Catholic, Orthodox and Protestant – are already in dialogue with men of other faiths and are, therefore, committed to accept its perils and promises is obvious. This must be said even while noting that we are at the beginning of this venture and that, therefore, expectations should not be raised which cannot soon be fulfilled, but which require patient nurturing of new relationships. Conditions that call for dialogue are to be found, however, not just in the countries of Asia and Africa, but also in the West. The presence of settled communities of other faiths in countries that have been traditionally Christian, large groups of migrant workers, thousands of foreign students and many teachers, people connected with international organizations, the 'yoga' schools and 'centres' of some of the religions of the East in the major cities of the world – all these cannot be ignored, particularly the impression they make on young people and those who reject the institutions of traditional Christianity.[8] Therefore, situations that demand dialogue are not just distant phenomena in some far-off corners of the East, but are actually present next door as challenges and opportunities.

Further, with great varieties in cultural background and historic situation, and highly complex attitudes towards the basic questions of life, there is not one single approach to dialogue, although some mutually acceptable frame of reference is essential. Christians themselves – Roman Catholic, Orthodox and Protestant – bring to dialogue different cultural heritages and theological traditions and, therefore, it would be most unwise to expect or demand from them unanimity on particular points. People of other faiths have their own approaches to dialogue. Some tend to enter into it on the basis of common human concerns which they feel need urgent co-operative attention. Others participate in it on the assumption of an acknowledged 'religious' dimension in life which, according to them, needs to be given priority. Still others, who feel uneasy about some of the consequences of secularization and who are deeply worried about the effects of technology on man's inner life, enter into dialogue in search of 'spiritual' resources to guide and shape the quality of human life. Whatever the differences of basis and approach to dialogue on the part of Christians and men of other faiths, answers to some of the vexed questions must be sought in the experience of dialogue itself and not by remaining outside it. Therefore, dialogue should take place in freedom. Without the freedom to be committed to one's own faith and to be open to that of another to witness, to change and to be changed, genuine dialogue would be impossible.

There is a further point that emerges out of the experience of dialogue which must not be forgotten. This is the element of the sinful and the demonic which is present in all human encounters. Therefore, no dialogue can ever be automatically 'successful'. A concrete example can be given here from India, where generally speaking, it is easy to have dialogue with Hindus. But twice in one year, plans made for a meeting between Hindus and Christians in a university town in North India, which is also a famous pilgrim centre, had to be cancelled. The following quotations from the letter of a Hindu friend indicate some of the reasons. Politely declining the Christian invitation, the Hindu friend wrote to his Christian *bhai* (brother): 'Do not think that I am against dialogue . . . On the contrary, I am fully convinced that dialogue is an essential part of human life, and therefore of religious life itself . . . Yet, to be frank with you, there is something which makes me uneasy in the way in which you Christians are now trying so eagerly to enter into official and formal dialogue with us. Have you already forgotten that what you call "inter-faith dialogue" is quite a new feature in your understanding and practice of Christianity? Until a few years ago, and often still today, your relations with us were confined, either to merely the social plane, or to preaching in order to convert us to your *dharma* . . . For all matters concerning *dharma* you were deadly against us, violently or stealthily according to cases. It was plain to see from your preaching to old Christians or prospective converts, or from your, at best, condescending attitude towards us in your pamphlets and magazines. And the pity was that your attacks and derogatory remarks were founded in sheer ignorance of what we really are, or what we believe and worship . . . The main obstacles to real dialogue are, on the one hand, a feeling of superiority and, on the other, the fear of losing one's identity.'[9]

These are strong words indeed, but they do indicate how fear and distrust can ruin the conditions for genuine dialogue and why openness and love are absolutely essential in our relationships. Some people of other faiths suspect that dialogue is simply a new and subtle Christian tool for mission that is being forged in the post-colonial era. On the other hand, there are some Christians who fear that dialogue with men of other faiths is a betrayal of mission and disobedience to the command to proclaim the Gospel. How do we express our obedience to Christ in truth and love, taking into account both these fears? The fear of losing one's identity is experienced not only by Christians, but also by men of other faiths. How do we bring together identity and community in these situations? None of these questions can be discussed in a purely academic way. It is in the living context of continuing dialogue that the meaning of identity should be sought. As Bishop Matthews remarks: 'An unseemly anxiety to preserve our heritage is to lose it and, at the same time, to attempt to limit God; but a willingness finally to risk even the loss of our heritage in the service of God and man is to find it. When there is a readiness to risk all, God may be trusted to be faithful in giving all back again in a renewed and enlarged perspective.'[10]

These matters lead us to the basic question to which reference was made in the very beginning of this address, viz. the imperative in the Christian faith that constrains us to enter into dialogue. Visser 't Hooft rightly remarks, 'The pluralistic world throws us all back on the primary source of our faith and forces us to take a new look at the world around us. Thus pluralism can provide a real opportunity for a new united witness of the whole Church of Christ in and to the whole world.'[11]

III

The fundamental question then is this, 'Why are we, as Christians, in dialogue with men of other faiths at all?' It is not enough to merely describe our recent engagements, or to give pragmatic reasons for our involvement in the common human concerns of contemporary history. These are, of course, important and provide the context for our obedience, but our concern in dialogue itself should not be determined by intermittent responses to the changing pressures of the world, but in obedience to the Lord and in accordance with the guidance of the Holy Spirit. 'A pilgrim people must maintain their differentia as pilgrims,' wrote D. T. Niles, 'but they must belong to the society among whom their journey is set.'[12] Dialogue is one of the crucial areas of relationships between Christians and men of other faiths today where sustained theological reflection must continue not in the isolation of academic discussions, but in the midst of our life together in the community where all are pilgrims on the high roads of modern life.

There are at least three theological reasons why dialogue is and ought to be a continuing Christian concern. First, God in Jesus Christ has himself entered into relationship with men of all faiths and all ages, offering the good news of salvation. The incarnation is God's dialogue with men. To be in dialogue is, therefore, to be part of God's continuing work among us and our fellow men. Second, the offer of a true community inherent in the Gospel, through forgiveness, reconciliation and a new creation, and of which the Church is a sign and a symbol, inevitably leads to dialogue. The freedom and love which Christ offers constrain us to be in fellowship with strangers so that all may become fellow citizens in the household of God. Third, there is the promise of Jesus Christ that the Holy Spirit will lead us into all truth. Since truth, in the Biblical understanding, is not propositional but relational, and is to be sought, not in the isolation of lonely meditation, but in the living, personal confrontation between God and man, and men and men, dialogue becomes one of the means of the quest for truth. And, because Christians cannot claim to have a monopoly of truth, we need to meet men of other faiths and ideologies as part of our trust in and obedience to the promise of Christ.

It is sometimes said that the word 'dialogue' is not found in the Bible and that, therefore, it lacks Biblical authority. However, there are quite a few other words in the contemporary ecumenical vocabulary which also are not found in the Bible. It has already been said that by dialogue we do not mean just detached, intellectual discourse. While the noun 'dialogue' itself is not found in the Bible, the warm relationships and the intense personal encounters suggested by the active verb are very much in evidence throughout the Bible. God's dealing with his people and the nations, the very relationship and obligations implied in the covenant both with Noah and with Abraham, the work of kings and judges, of prophets and priests, the book of Job, the writings of the prophets and some of the Psalms where people talk back and forth to God – surely these do not suggest a one-way traffic of monologues from on high. In the New Testament too, where we see different ways in which our Lord deals with people, the way of dialogue is not contrary to the spirit in which he dealt with Nicodemus, the Samaritan woman, the centurion and his own disciples throughout his ministry. There are occasions, of course, when he refuses to be drawn into discussions and when his presence divides people and, therefore, one should not overdo this and claim that everything in the Bible is dialogue. But the Bible gives considerable support to those who do not wish to be theological bull-dozers trying to push through the jungle of religions, and seeking to flatten mountains of ideologies.

Therefore, there are sound theological reasons why dialogue should be a continuing Christian concern. The basis on which Christians enter into and continue their dialogue with others is their faith in Jesus Christ, the Son of God, who has become man on behalf of all men, of all ages and of all cultures. He is 'the true light that enlightens every man' (John 1:9), he is the Word become flesh 'full of grace and truth' (John 1:14); he is the one through whom God 'was reconciling the world to himself' (2 Corinthians 5:19); he is the one who became obedient unto death, 'even the death on a cross' and therefore was 'highly exalted (Philippians 2:8f.); and through him has God made known the mystery of his will 'to unite all things in him, things in heaven and things on earth' (Ephesians 1:10). It is Christology not 'comparative religion' that is the basis of our concern. Our primary interest is not in 'inter-religious conferences'; it is to be with Christ in his continuing work among men of all faiths and ideologies. Christ draws us out of our isolation into closer relationship with all men. In his name people have gone to the ends of the earth as humble participants in his continuing redeeming activity in history. He releases us from all kinds of bondage, including bondage to the safety of the group which shares the same faith, in order to enter into full and free relationship with others. Faith in Jesus Christ involves a way of life that demands obedience as well as a view of life that influences our understanding of God, our neighbours and the world of nature and history of which we are an inextricable part. Christian participation in dialogue is, therefore, part of the concrete living out of the view of life and the way of life that stem from faith in Jesus Christ. 'It is *because* of faith in God through Jesus Christ and *because* of our belief in the reality of Creation, the offer of Redemption, and the love of God shown in the Incarnation that we seek a positive relationship with men of other faiths.'[13]

Further, there is another aspect to the imperative of the Christian faith, which undergirds and directs the quest for community through dialogue. One of the historic consequences of the ministry of Jesus Christ – his life, death and resurrection – is the coming into being of the Christian Church, a community of people bound in fellowship to each other through faith in him. Working for and building up human communities is never easy, because of the persistence of sin in all structures of human life. When, in multi-religious societies, religious boundaries are sanctified and perpetuated by tradition, religions themselves become walls of separation rather than bridges of understanding between people. Therefore, the quest for community today cuts across these boundaries, and persons of different faiths reach out to form new communities of greater freedom and love. One of the ways in which Christians can be deeply involved in this struggle is through dialogue. Therefore, dialogue should not be regarded as just a hurried, post-colonial attempt to rub off the smell of colonialism that is still sticking to most of us. Neither is it a tool to show that we identify ourselves with our neighbours through talking about their faiths and quoting their Scriptures. Still less should it be considered as merely an emotional reaction to a triumphalistic understanding of mission in the past. It is more than that; it is the expression of our faith in Jesus Christ in and through life in the community. 'Christ is our peace, who has made us both one, and has broken down the dividing wall of hostility . . . for through him we both have access in one Spirit to the Father. So then you are no longer strangers and sojourners, but you are fellow citizens with the saints and members of the household of God', says the apostle (Ephesians 2:14, 18f.). For Christians, the fight against all that destroys true community, the quest for spiritual resources to undergird all efforts to build community, and the search for the ultimate meaning of truly human existence in community, cannot be separated from faith in Jesus Christ. Therefore, Christians must at all times be actively involved in building up a truly universal community of freedom and love.

A further point that needs to be recognized here is our faith in the promise of Jesus Christ about the Holy Spirit.

'When the Spirit of truth comes, he will guide you into all truth; for he will not speak on his own authority, but whatever he hears he will speak, and he will declare to you the things that are to come' (John 16:13). This promise not only makes it necessary for us to enter into dialogue, but also to continue in it without fear, but with full expectation and openness. It is not claimed that dialogue is the only way in this quest for truth; nor is it forgotten that discovery of truth is not inevitable. Possibilities of error, distortion and confusion are as present in situations of dialogue as in any human situation. Therefore, one must recognize that there is no guarantee that all dialogues shall automatically lead the participants into fuller truth. But the way in which truth is revealed, understood and communicated in the Bible makes it clear that one should look for 'things that are to come' in the areas of personal relationships with God and our fellow men. Dialogue with men of other faiths and ideologies can, therefore, be regarded as at least one of the possibilities open to those who are willing to undertake the journey. Those who fear that the train of truth might be in danger of derailment should note that obedience to truth already revealed in Jesus Christ and trust in his promises outweigh the risks that are present in all human adventures. Our hope in dialogue lies in the continuing work of the Holy Spirit in judgement, in mercy and in new creation.

At this hour of history when the destinies of all people everywhere – and not only of Christians – are being drawn together as never before, and when, because of the massive power of impersonal forces, the need to recognize the ultimate source of man's personal being and community life is so urgent, dialogue offers a helpful opportunity for the renewal of that truly religious quest which Christians believe to be fulfilled by God in Jesus Christ. Therefore, Christians cannot and should not at this juncture withdraw from dialogue; on the contrary, there is every reason to continue in it, to extend it and to deepen it. However, it is only through the guidance of the Holy Spirit, who may lead us into areas as yet strange and unfamiliar to us, and through obedience to Jesus Christ, the crucified and risen Lord, which may mean joining the traffic across the borders beyond which we have not ventured so far, that the continuing Christian dialogue can remain truly faithful dialogue.

1. See *Edinburgh 1910*: An Account and Interpretation of the World Missionary Conference by W. H. T. Gairdner, London, 1910 – two sections, Chapter VII, Carrying the Gospel to all the non-Christian World, pp. 68ff., and Chapter X, The Missionary Message in relation to the non-Christian Religions, pp. 134ff. *The Christian Message: Jerusalem Report*, Vol. I, Oxford University Press, London, 1928, deals with 'the value of religious values in non-Christian religions' on pp. 417ff. and 'Secular Civilization and the Christian Faith' on pp. 284ff. *The Authority of Faith*, Vol. I, International Missionary Council, 1939, Papers and Findings of the Madras Meeting; see particularly Findings, pp. 169ff.
2. *New Delhi Report*, SCM Press, London, 1961, Section III, Witness, p. 84.
3. *The Uppsala Report 1968*, World Council of Churches, Geneva, 1968, p. 29.
4. *The Documents of Vatican II*, Guild Press, New York, 1966, pp. 660ff.
5. The following meetings are referred to in the text: Christian-Hindu, Kottayam, India, 14–16 October 1962; Christian-Muslim, Birmingham, UK, 27–28 January 1968; Christian-Jewish, Lugano, Switzerland, 27–30 October 1970; Christian-Buddhist-Confucian, Seoul, Korea, 8–19 October 1967; World Conference on Religion and Peace,

Kyoto, Japan, 16–22 October 1970; and Hindu, Buddhist, Christian and Muslim, Ajaltoun, Lebanon, 16–25 March 1970.

6. M. M. Thomas, *Religion and Society*, Bangalore, Vol. IX, No. 3, September 1962, pp. 2ff.
7. *Study Encounter*, Vol. VI, No. 2, 1970, pp. 97–106.
8. There are about 600,000 Muslims in Canada and the United States, 120,000 of them clustered around New York City. The Federation of Islamic Associations in the USA and Canada has planned a sixteen-million-dollar culture centre in New York City (Religious News Service, New York, 15 July 1969, p. 10). There are about 500,000 Buddhists in the USA, 8000 in Germany and 5000 in England (article by Harry Thomsen, 'Non-Buddhist Buddhism and Non-Christian Christianity in Japan' in *Syncretism*, (Ed.) Sven S. Hartman, Almqvist & Wiksell, Stockholm, 1969, p. 128). In certain parts of Britain, with communities of Hindus, Buddhists, Muslims and Sikhs living with Christian neighbours, the question of religious education in schools has now become more complicated. (See *Learning for Living, a Journal of Christian Education*, London, January 1969, Vol. 8, No. 3, article by Mrs Teresina Havens, PhD, p. 31, and *World Faith*, London, No. 81, August 1970, Statement on Religious Education, p. 20f.)
9. *Dialogue between Men of Living Faiths*, WCC Geneva, 1971, pp. 22ff.
10. James K. Matthews, *A Church Truly Catholic*, New York, 1969, p. 160.
11. *Ecumenical Review*, Vol. XVIII, April 1966, No. 2, article 'Pluralism, Temptation or Opportunity?', p. 149.
12. D. T. Niles, *Upon the Earth*, Lutterworth, London, 1962, p. 79.
13. *International Review of Mission*, Vol. LIX, No. 236, October 1970, theme: Faithful Dialogue, p. 384.

9. 'WHATEVER PATH MEN CHOOSE IS MINE'

John Hick

For many of us in the West the relation between Christianity and the other world religions has until recently been a rather theoretical issue to which rather theoretical responses have seemed sufficient. We have lived within the cultural borders of Christendom and – many of us – within the ecclesiastical borders of the Church. From this centre we – that is, our forebears, and still the Church today – have been sending out missionaries into all the continents of the earth, and have enjoyed a vague sense that the world is, however tardily, in process of becoming Christianized. And so we have in the past generally thought of the non-Christian world in negative terms, as the unfortunate not-yet-Christianized portion of humanity and as potential recipients of the divine grace which is coming through the evangelists whom we send out to them.

However, several things have happened to shatter this attitude of religious imperialism.

One has been the growing awareness, produced by the news media and by travel, of the sheer size and religious variety of mankind outside our own Anglo-Saxon tribe. The estimated Christian population of the world is 983·6 million, constituting just under a quarter of the world's total population of 4123·9 million (*Encyclopedia Britannica 1978 Book of the Year*, p. 616). But whilst the total number of Christians is slowly rising, the proportion of Christians is slowly declining, because the explosion in the human population (the number of which will have roughly doubled between 1970 and about 2005) is taking place more rapidly outside Christendom than within it. Thus the Christian faith is held today, as in the past, only by a minority of the human race; and it looks as though this minority may well be smaller rather than larger in the future. This thought casts a massive shadow over any assumption that it is God's will that all mankind shall be converted to the Christian faith.

Again, it is a fact evident to ordinary people (even though not always taken into account by theologians) that in the great majority of cases – say, 98 or 99 per cent – the religion in which a person believes and to which he adheres depends upon where he was born. That is to say, if someone is born to Muslim parents in Egypt or Pakistan, that person is very likely to be a Muslim; if to Buddhist parents in Sri Lanka or Burma, that person is very likely to be a Buddhist; if to Hindu parents in India, that person is very likely to be a Hindu; if to Christian parents in Europe or the Americas, that person is very likely to be a Christian. Of course in each case he may be a fully committed or a merely nominal adherent of his religion. But whether one is a Christian, a Jew, a Muslim, a Buddhist, a Sikh, a Hindu – or for that matter a Marxist or a Maoist – depends nearly always on the part of the world in which one happens to have been born. Any credible religious faith must be able to make sense of this circumstance. And a credible Christian faith must make sense of it by relating it to the universal sovereignty and fatherhood of God. This is rather conspicuously not done by the older theology which held that God's saving activity is confined within a single narrow thread of human life, namely that recorded in our own scriptures.

Another factor making for change is that the old unflattering caricatures of other religions are now being replaced by knowledge based on serious objective study. Our bookshops now carry shelves of good popular as well as technical works on the history of religion, the phenomenology of religion, and the comparative study of religions; and only one who prefers to be ignorant can any longer complacently congratulate himself upon knowing nothing about other faiths. It is no longer acceptable to plead ignorance concerning the wider religious life of mankind as an excuse for parochial theological prejudices. Times have changed and today no one wishes to present the eighteenth-century image of Fielding's Parson Thwackum who said, 'When I mention religion, I mean the Christian religion; and not only the Christian religion, but the Protestant religion; and not only the Protestant religion, but the Church of England.'

And, perhaps most importantly of all, since the 1950s Asian immigration from India, Pakistan and (as it now is) Bangladesh has brought sizeable Muslim, Hindu and Sikh communities to many of our cities, adding three more non-Christian groups to the Jews who had already been there for more than two centuries. By their very existence these non-Christian communities presented the Church with a number of new questions, which it has generally chosen to see as difficult problems. Should we try to help the Muslims, Sikhs and Hindus to find suitable premises in which to worship? Should we be willing to sell them redundant church buildings? Should local religious broadcasting include or exclude them? Should we try to insist that all children in the state schools shall receive Christian religious instruction, regardless of the religion which they or their parents profess? And so on. These questions all have theological implications, and have helped to turn the attention of Christians to the problem of the relation of Christianity to the other world religions.

When you visit the various non-Christian places of worship in one of our big cities you discover – possibly with a shock of surprise – that phenomenologically (or in other words, to human observation) the same kind of thing is taking place in them as in a Christian church. That is to say, human beings are coming together to open their minds to a higher reality, which is thought of as the personal creator and Lord of the universe, and as making vital moral demands upon the lives of men and women. Of course the trappings are very different – in a church men wear shoes and no hat; in mosque, gurdwara and temple, a hat and no shoes; in a synagogue, both. In some you sit on a pew, in others on the floor. In some there is singing, in others there is not. Different musical instruments or none are used. More importantly, the supreme being is referred to as God in a Christian church, as Adonai in a Jewish synagogue, as Allah in a Muslim mosque, as Param Atma in a Sikh gurdwara, as Rama or as Krishna in a Hindu temple. And yet there is an important sense in which what is being done in the several forms of worship is essentially the same.

In the Jewish synagogue God is worshipped as maker of heaven and earth and the God of Abraham and Isaac and Jacob, who led the children of Israel out of Egypt into the promised land and who has called them to live as a light to lighten the world. Worship is very close in form and ethos to Christian worship in the Protestant traditions. Here is a passage of typical Jewish prayer:

> With a great love have You loved us, O Lord our God, and with exceeding compassion have You pitied us. Our Father and King, our fathers trusted in You, and You

> taught them the laws of life: be gracious also to us, and teach us. Have compassion upon us, and guide us, our Merciful Father, that we may grasp and understand, learn and teach, observe and uphold with love all the words of Your law.[1]

In Muslim mosques God is worshipped as the maker of heaven and earth, and as the sovereign Lord of the Universe, omnipotent, holy and merciful, before whom men bow in absolute submission. Here is a typical passage of Muslim prayer:

> Praise be to God, Lord of creation,
> Source of all livelihood, who orders the morning.
> Lord of majesty and honour, of grace and beneficence.
> He who is so far that he may not be seen
>   and so near that he witnesses the secret things.
> Blessed be He and for ever exalted.[2]

Or again:

> To God belongs the praise, Lord of the heavens and Lord of the earth, the Lord of all being. His is the dominion in the heavens and in the earth: he is the Almighty, the All-wise.[3]

In Sikh Gurdwaras God is worshipped as the maker of heaven and earth, the gracious lord of time and eternity, who demands righteousness and seeks peace and goodwill between men. Here is the Sikh morning prayer which is at the same time a creed:

> There is but one God. He is all that is.
> He is the Creator of all things and He is all-Pervasive.

He is without fear and without enmity.
He is timeless, unborn and self-existent.
He is the Enlightener
And can be realized by grace of Himself alone.
He was in the beginning; He was in all ages.
The True One is, was, [O Nanak,] and shall forever be.[4]

The Hindu temples which have been established in Britain represent the *bhakti* or theistic-devotional form of Hinduism. In them God is worshipped as the ultimate Lord of all, the infinite divine Life known under many aspects and names. Against the background of throbbing music the name of God is chanted again and again by ecstatic worshippers. The language of *bhakti* devotion is emotional and personal. Here is a typical Vaishnavite hymn:

O save me, save me, Mightiest,
Save me and set me free.
O let the love that fills my breast
Cling to thee lovingly.

Grant me to taste how sweet thou art;
Grant me but this, I pray,
And never shall my love depart
Or turn from thee away.

Then I thy name shall magnify
And tell thy praise abroad,
For very love and gladness I
Shall dance before my God.[5]

And here is a verse expressing the Hindu idea of the many incarnations of God:

Seers and sages, saints and hermits, fix on Him their
reverent gaze,
And in faint and trembling accents, holy scripture hymns
His praise.
He the omnipresent spirit, Lord of heaven and earth and
hell,
To redeem His people, freely has vouchsafed with men
to dwell.[6]

In the light of the phenomenological similarity of worship in these different traditions we have to ask whether people in church, synagogue, mosque, gurdwara and temple are worshipping different Gods or are worshipping the same God? Are Adonai and God, Allah and Param Atma, Rama and Krishna different Gods, or are these different names for the same ultimate Being?

There would seem to be three possibilities. One is that there exist, ontologically, many gods. But this conflicts with the belief concerning each that he is the creator or the source of the world. A second possibility is that one faith-community, let us say our own, worships God whilst the others vainly worship images which exist only in their imaginations. But even within Christianity itself, is there not a variety of overlapping mental images of God – for example, as stern judge and predestinating power, and as gracious and loving heavenly Father – so that different Christian groups, and even different Christian individuals, are worshipping the divine Being through their different images of him? And do not the glimpses which I have just offered of worship within the various religious traditions suggest that our Christian images overlap with many non-Christian images of God? If so, a third possibility must seem the most probable, namely that there is but one God, who is maker and lord of all; that in his infinite fullness and richness of being he exceeds all our human attempts to grasp him in thought; and that the devout in the various great world religions are in fact worshipping that one God, but through different, overlapping concepts or mental images of him.

If this is so, the older Christian view of other faiths as areas of spiritual darkness within which there is no salvation, no knowledge of God, and no acceptable worship must be mistaken. This older view, which few still entertain in practice today, was enshrined in the traditional Roman Catholic dogma, *extra ecclesiam nulla salus* (outside the Church no salvation). To quote a classic utterance from this point of view, the Council of Florence in 1438–45 declared that 'no one remaining outside the Catholic Church, not just pagans, but also Jews or heretics or schismatics, can become partakers of eternal life; but they will go to the everlasting fire which was prepared for the devil and his angels, unless before the end of life they are joined to the church'.[7] The Protestant missionary equivalent, which likewise is entertained by few today, is the doctrine that outside Christianity there is no salvation. As a fairly recent expression of this, the Congress on World Mission at Chicago in 1960 declared, 'In the years since the war, more than one billion souls have passed into eternity and more than half of these went to the torment of hell fire without even hearing of Jesus Christ, who He was, or why He died on the cross of Calvary.'[8]

This older view has come to seem increasingly implausible and unrealistic in the light of growing knowledge of other faiths and as a result of better contacts with their adherents. Consequently Christian theologians, perhaps most notably within the Roman communion, have been making strenuous efforts to escape from the unacceptable implications of the older view, though usually without feeling entitled explicitly to renounce it. This is, of course, in accordance with the established ecclesiastical method of developing and changing doctrine. One cannot say that a formerly proclaimed dogma was wrong, but one can reinterpret it to mean something very different from what it was originally understood to mean. Such exercises often display a high level of ingenuity; though no amount of intellectual sophistication can save them from seeming slightly ridiculous or slightly dishonest to the outsider. At any rate, in the attempt to retain the dogma of no salvation outside the Church, or outside Christianity, we have the ideas of implicit, as distinguished from explicit, faith; of baptism by desire, as distinguished from literal baptism; and as a Protestant equivalent, the idea of the latent Church as distinguished from the manifest Church; and, again, the suggestion that men can only come to God through Jesus Christ but that those who have not encountered him in this life will encounter him in the life to come.

Or again there is Karl Rahner's notion of the anonymous Christian.[9] The devout Muslim, or Hindu, or Sikh, or Jew can be regarded as an anonymous Christian, this being an honorary status granted unilaterally to people who have not expressed any desire for it. Or again there is the claim that Christianity, properly understood, is not a religion but is a revelation which judges and supersedes all religions. Or finally there is Hans Küng's distinction between the ordinary way of salvation in the world religions and the extraordinary way in the Church. Küng says, 'A man is to be saved within the religion that is made available to him in his historical situation. Hence it is his right and duty to seek God within that religion in which the hidden God has already found him.' Thus the world religions are, he says, 'the way of salvation in universal salvation history;

the general way of salvation, we can even say, for the people of the world religions: the more common, the "ordinary" way of salvation, as against which the way of salvation in the Church appears as something very special and extraordinary'.[10] This sounds at first extremely promising. However, Küng goes on to take away with one hand what he has given with the other. The ordinary way of salvation for the majority of mankind in the world religions turns out to be only an interim way until, sooner or later, they come to an explicit Christian faith. The people of the world religions are, he says, 'pre-Christian, directed towards Christ . . . The men of the world religions are not professing Christians but, by the grace of God, they are called and marked out to be Christians' (Neuner, pp. 55–6).[11] One is reminded of the British amnesty for illegal immigrants. Although they are unauthorized entrants into the Kingdom of Heaven, the Indian and Pakistani and other foreign worshippers of God will be accepted if sooner or later they come forward to be legally registered by Christian baptism!

Thus all of these thinkers, who are trying so hard to find room for their non-Christian brethren in the sphere of salvation, are still working within the presuppositions of the old dogma. Only Christians can be saved; so we have to say that devout and godly non-Christians are really, in some metaphysical sense, Christians or Christians-to-be without knowing it. Although to the ordinary non-ecclesiastical mind this borders upon double-talk, yet in intention it is a charitable extension of the sphere of grace to people who had formerly been regarded as beyond the pale. As such it can function as a psychological bridge between the no longer acceptable older view and the new view which is emerging. But sooner or later we have to get off the bridge on to the other side. We have to make what might be called a Copernican revolution in our theology of religions. You will remember that the old Ptolemaic astronomy held that the earth is the centre of the solar system and that all the other heavenly bodies revolve around it. And when it was realized that this theory did not fit the observed facts, particularly the wandering movements of the planets, epicycles were added, circles revolving on circles to complicate the theory and bring it nearer to the facts. By analogy the 'no salvation outside Christianity' doctrine is theologically Ptolemaic. Christianity is seen as the centre of the universe of faiths, and all the other religions are regarded as revolving round it and as being graded in value according to their distance from it. And the theories of implicit faith, baptism by desire, anonymous Christianity, the latent Church, the 'ordinary' and 'extraordinary' ways of salvation, and the claim that the Christian religion is not a religion whereas all the others are, are so many epicycles added to this Ptolemaic theology to try to accommodate our growing knowledge of other faiths and our awareness of the true piety and devotion which they sustain.

It is worth noting that just as a Ptolemaic astronomy could be developed, not only from the standpoint of this earth, but from any of the other planets, so also a Ptolemaic theology can be developed not only from a Christian standpoint but equally from the standpoint of any other faith. From, let us say, a Hindu centre one could say that devout Christians are implicit Hindus in virtue of their sincere desire for the truth even though they do not yet know what the truth is; that other faiths provide the 'ordinary way' of salvation whilst Hinduism is the 'extraordinary' way, in which the truth is manifest which in the others is latent; that Hinduism is not a religion but the eternal truth judging and superseding all religions. The

Ptolemaic stance can be taken by anyone. But it can only serve as an interim position whilst we prepare our minds for a Copernican revolution. Copernicus realized that it is the sun, and not the earth, that is at the centre, and that all the heavenly bodies, including our own earth, revolve around it. And we have to realize that the universe of faiths centres upon *God*, and not upon Christianity or upon any other religion. He is the sun, the originative source of light and life, whom all the religions reflect in their own different ways.

This must mean that the different world religions have each served as God's means of revelation to and point of contact with a different stream of human life. Such a conclusion makes sense of the history of religions. The first period was one in which the innate religiousness of the human mind expressed itself in the different forms of what we can call natural religion – the worship of spirits, ancestors, nature gods, and often bloodthirsty national deities. But about 900 or 800 B.C. there began what Karl Jaspers[12] has called the axial period in which seminal moments of religious experience occurred in each of the four principal centres of civilization – Greece, the Near East, India, and China – out of which the higher religions have come. In this immensely rich and important band of time the great Hebrew prophets lived; in Persia, Zoroaster; in China, Confucius and the author (or authors) of the Taoist Scriptures; in India, the Buddha, and Mahavira, and the writers of the Upanishads and of the Bhagavad Gita; in Greece, Pythagoras, Socrates and Plato. And then later, out of the stream of prophetic religion established by the Hebrew prophets there came Jesus and the rise of Christianity, and Mohammad and the rise of Islam.

Now in this axial period, some two and a half thousand years ago, communication between the continents and civilizations of the earth was so slow that for all practical purposes men lived in different cultural worlds. There could not be a divine revelation, through any human means, to mankind as a whole, but only separate revelations within the different streams of human history. And so it is a natural and indeed an inevitable hypothesis that God, the ultimate divine reality, was in this axial period revealing his presence and his will to mankind through a number of specially sensitive and responsive spirits. In each case the revelatory experiences, and the religious traditions to which they gave rise, were conditioned by the history, culture, language, climate, and indeed all the concrete circumstances of human life at that particular time and place. Thus the cultural and philosophical form of the revelation of the divine is characteristically different in each case, although we may believe that everywhere the one divine Spirit has been at work, pressing in upon the human spirit.

I shall return presently to this historical view of the different religious traditions to ask what difference it makes that the world has now become a communicational unity. But let me first ask the question that is so important to us as Christians, namely, what does all this imply concerning the person of our Lord? What about the uniqueness of Christ, the belief that Jesus was God incarnate, the second Person of the Holy Trinity become man, the eternal Logos made flesh? Did he not say, 'I and the Father are one', and 'No one comes to the Father, but by me'? Here, unfortunately, we have to enter the realm of New Testament criticism: and I say 'unfortunately' because of the notorious uncertainties of this realm. There are powerful schools of thought, following fashions which tend to change from generation to generation, but no consensus either across the years or across the schools.

But this at least can be said: that whereas until some three or four generations ago it was generally accepted among biblical scholars that Jesus claimed to be the Son of God, with a unique consciousness of oneness with the Heavenly Father, so that the doctrine of the Incarnation was believed to be firmly based in the consciousness and teaching of Jesus himself, today this is no longer generally held and is indeed very widely thought not to be the case. I am not going to enter into a detailed discussion of the New Testament evidence: I am neither competent to do this, nor is there time. I will only quote some summarizing words of Wolfhart Pannenberg in his massive work, *Jesus: God and Man* (SCM Press, London, 1968), where he says that 'After D. F. Strauss and F. C. Bauer, John's Gospel could no longer be claimed uncritically as a historical source of authentic words of Jesus. Consequently, other concepts and titles that were more indirectly connected with Jesus's relation to God came into the foreground of the question of Jesus's "Messianic self-consciousness'. However, the transfer of these titles to Jesus . . . has been demonstrated with growing certainty by critical study of the Gospels to be the work of the post-Easter community. Today it must be taken as all but certain that the pre-Easter Jesus neither designated himself as Messiah (or Son of God) nor accepted such a confession to him from others' (p. 327). Not all New Testament scholars would endorse Pannenberg's words. But certainly one can no longer regard it as a fact proved out of the New Testament that Jesus thought of himself as God incarnate. On the contrary, this now seems to be very unlikely. And certainly we cannot rest anything on the assumption that the great christological sayings of the Fourth Gospel (such as 'I and my Father are one') were ever spoken, in sober historical fact, by the Jesus who walked the hills and villages of

Galilee. It seems altogether more probable that they reflect the developing theology of the Church at about the end of the first century.

Now if Jesus himself did not think of himself as God Incarnate, one might well ask whether his disciples ought to do so. But instead of pursuing that question directly it seems more profitable to accept that the Son-of-God and God-Incarnate language has become deeply entrenched in the discourse of Christian thought and piety, and to ask what *kind* of language it is. Is the statement that Jesus was God Incarnate, or the Son of God, or God the Son, a statement of literal fact?; and if so, what precisely is the fact? Or is it a poetic, or symbolic, or mythological statement? It can, I think, only be the latter. It can hardly be a literal factual statement, since after nearly 2000 years of Christian reflection no factual content has been discerned in it. Unless, that is, we give it factual content in terms of the idea of Jesus's Virgin Birth. We could then say that his being the Son of God means that the Holy Spirit fulfilled the role of the male parent in his conception. But he would then be a divine-human figure such as is familiar from Greek mythology; for example, Hercules, whose father was the god Jupiter and whose mother was a human woman. However, this has never seriously been regarded as the real meaning of the doctrine of the Incarnation. What then is its real meaning? Whenever in the history of Christian thought theologians have tried to spell out its meaning in literal, factual terms the result has been heretical. A classic example would be Apollinarius's theory that Jesus's body and soul were human but that his spirit was the eternal divine Logos. This was rejected as heresy because it implied that Jesus was not genuinely human. And all attempts to treat the Incarnation as a factual hypothesis have likewise been rejected by the Church because they have failed to do justice either to Jesus's full humanity or to his full deity. Indeed, one may say that the fundamental heresy is precisely to treat the Incarnation as a factual hypothesis! For the reason why it has never been possible to state a literal meaning for the idea of Incarnation is simply that it has no literal meaning. It is a mythological idea, a figure of speech, a piece of poetic imagery. It is a way of saying that Jesus is our living contact with the transcendent God. In his presence we find that we are brought into the presence of God. We believe that he is so truly God's servant that in living as his disciples we are living according to the divine purpose. And as our sufficient and saving point of contact with God there is for us something absolute about him which justifies the absolute language which Christianity has developed. Thus reality is being expressed mythologically when we say that he is the Son of God, God Incarnate, the Logos made flesh.

When we see the Incarnation as a mythological idea applied to Jesus to express the experienced fact that he is our sufficient, effective and saving point of contact with God, we no longer have to draw the negative conclusion that he is man's one and only effective point of contact with God. We can revere Christ as the one through whom we have found salvation, without having to deny other points of reported saving contact between God and man. We can commend the way of Christian faith without having to discommend other ways of faith. We can say that there is salvation in Christ without having to say that there is no salvation other than in Christ.

Let us return, finally, to the historical situation. We have seen that the great world religions arose within different streams of human life and have in the past flowed down the centuries within different cultural channels. They have until recently interacted with one another only spasmodically, and nearly always in hostile clashes rather than in mutual dialogue and friendly interpenetration. But latterly this situation has been changing radically. Since the late nineteenth century there has been a positive influence of Christianity upon Hinduism, bearing fruit in a new social concern in India; and an influence of both Hinduism and Buddhism upon Christianity, bearing fruit in the new Western appreciation of meditation and the arts of spiritual self-development. And today the world religions are increasingly in contact with one another in conscious dialogue and in deliberate attempts to learn about and to learn from one another. These mutual influences can only increase in the future. It is I think very important to notice that each of the world religions is in practice an on-going history of change. Each likes to think of itself as immutable, the same yesterday, today and for ever. But the historian can see that this is not so. Each of the major world faiths has gone through immense historical developments, revolutions and transformations. Each has experienced both times of rapid change, in sudden expansions, schisms, reformations and renaissances, and also periods of relative stability. Islam has perhaps changed less than the others; but even within Islam there have been immense evolutionary developments and also the growth of important divisions. Hinduism has always been able to change, and to absorb new influences into its own life. Christianity and Buddhism have both developed through the centuries almost out of recognition. And in each case there is in principle no limit to the further developments that may take place in the future. In the next period these will occur in a context of interaction. The future of Christianity will be formed partly by influences stemming from Hinduism, Buddhism, and

Islam; and so also, in a mutually interactive system, with the other world faiths. And all partly also by influences stemming from the secular civilization within which they will all exist.

Can we peer into the future and anticipate the pattern of development? Obviously, in trying to do so we are guessing. However, such guessing is today dignified by the name of Futurology and large books are written about the state of the planet in, say, the year 2000. These speculations are not random guesses, but are based on the projection of present trends, together with the foreseeable emergence of new trends. If secular seers can speculate in these ways about the future of man, why should we not try to consider the forms which the religious life of mankind will take in, say, a hundred years' time if the present basic trends continue? I am making the very major assumption, which there is no time here to defend, that man's religiousness is innate and that religion will continue in some form so long as human nature remains essentially the same. But what forms will it take? The broad trend of the present century is ecumenical. Old divisions are being transcended. The deeper essentials in which people agree are tending to seem more important than the matters on which they differ. Projecting this trend into the future we may suppose that the ecumenical spirit which has already so largely transformed Christianity will increasingly affect the relations between the world faiths. There may well be a growing world ecumenism, in which the common commitment of faith in a higher spiritual reality which demands brotherhood on earth will seem more and more significant, whilst the differences between the religious traditions will seem proportionately less significant. The relation between them may thus become somewhat like that between the Christian denominations in Britain – that is to say, they are on increasingly friendly speaking terms; they freely visit one another's worship and are beginning to be able to share places of worship; they co-operate in all sorts of service to the community; their clergy are accustomed to meet together for discussion, and there is even a degree of interchange of ministries; and so on.

What we are picturing here as a future possibility is not a single world religion, but a situation in which the different traditions no longer see themselves and each other as rival ideological communities. A single world religion is, I would think, never likely, and not a consummation to be desired. For so long as there is a variety of human types there will be a variety of kinds of worship and a variety of theological emphases and approaches. There will always be the more mystical and the more prophetic types of faith, with their corresponding awareness of the ultimate Reality as non-personal and as personal. There will always be the more spontaneous, warm and Spirit-filled forms of devotion, and the more liturgical, orderly and rationally controlled forms. There will always be the more vivid consciousness of the divine as gracious love, and as infinite demand and judgement, and so on. But it is not necessary, and it may in a more ecumenical age not be felt to be necessary, to assume that if God is being truly worshipped by Christians he cannot also be being truly worshipped by Jews and Muslims and Sikhs and by theistic Hindus and Amida Buddhists; or even that if the Ultimate Divine Reality is being validly experienced within the theistic streams of religious life as a personal presence, that Reality may not also be validly experienced within other streams of religious life as the infinite Being-Consciousness-Bliss (*Satchitananda*) of some forms of Hinduism, or as the ineffable cosmic Buddha-nature (the *Dharmakaya*) of some forms of Buddhism.

Let me then end with a quotation from one of the great revelatory scriptures of the world: 'Howsoever man may approach me, even so do I accept them; for, on all sides, whatever path they may choose is mine.'[13]

1. From the Weekday Morning Service in *Service of the Heart: Weekday Sabbath and Festival Services and Prayer, for Home and Synagogue*, Union of Liberal and Progressive Synagogues, London, 1967, pp. 40f.
2. *Alive to God, Muslim and Christian Prayer*, ed. Kenneth Cragg, Oxford University Press, London, 1970, p. 65.
3. *Ibid.*, p. 61.
4. Harbans Singh, *Guru Nanak and the Origins of the Sikh Faith*, Asia Publishing House, London, 1969, pp. 96f.
5. A. C. Bouquet, ed., *Sacred Books of the World*, Pelican Books, London, 1954, p. 246.
6. *Ibid.*, p. 226.
7. Denzinger, *Enchiridion Symbolorum Definitionum et Declarationum de Rebus Fidei et Morum*, 29th edition, Freiburg, 1952, No. 714.
8. *Facing the Unfinished Task*, ed. J. O. Percy, Eerdmans, Grand Rapids, Michigan, 1961, p. 9.
9. *Theological Investigations*, Vol. 5, Darton, Longman and Todd, London, 1966, chapter 6. His most recent discussion, reaffirming the notion, occurs in *Theological Investigations*, Vol. 14, 1976, chapter 17.
10. *Christian Revelation and World Religions*, ed. Joseph Neuner, Burns & Oates, London, 1967, pp. 52f.
11. For Küng's more recent views see his *On Being A Christian*, Doubleday, New York, 1976, and Collins, London, 1977, A. III.
12. *The Origin and Goal of History*, Karl Jaspers, Routledge and Kegan Paul, London, 1953.
13. *Bhagavad Gita, IV, 11.* On the interpretation of this verse see R. C. Zaehner, *The Bhagavad Gita*, The Clarendon Press, Oxford, 1969, pp. 185f.

10. CHRISTIANITY AND THE WORLD RELIGIONS

Jürgen Moltmann

Having given an account of the special relationship of Christ's Church to Israel, we must now (while constantly revising our bearings in the light of this relationship) investigate the relations of the Christian faith to the world religions. The Church's abiding origin in Israel, its permanent orientation to Israel's hope, Christianity's resulting special vocation to prepare the way for the coming kingdom in history – all this will also give its stamp to the dialogue with the world religions.[1] The dialogue cannot be determined by arbitrary and predetermined attitudes, but only by attitudes and judgements which are based on Christianity's special promise and are directed towards the universal future of mankind in the kingdom of God. But just because of this we must note the changed world situation in which the world religions find themselves today and to which they are adapting themselves.

THE NEW WORLD SITUATION

At one time every nation, every civilization and every religion on earth had its own history, its particular origin and its own future. History only existed in the plural form of all the different histories on earth. There was no world history – merely human histories in the world. Today nations, civilizations and religions unavoidably enter a 'single, common world'. The economic, military, political and social web of interdependencies and communications is growing visibly. With the increasing density of the interweaving, the present conflicts are becoming a general threat. Because this general threat can only be overcome by common efforts, there is a demand for new community. With this the quality of history is changing too; it is making a leap, as it were, into something new: the nations will continue to have their pasts and their traditions in the plural, but their future and their hope will now only exist in the singular. This means that the future of the nations is a *single* humanity. Either the nations will run aground on their divisions or they will survive in new community. Consequently survival in the future will no longer be by the unaltered prolongation of national, cultural and religious pasts: it is something new, because it can only be what is in common. It has to be what is in common if mankind is still to win through to a future. The phrase 'world religion' has hitherto been understood to cover the great supranational 'higher' religions, Buddhism, Hinduism, Confucianism, Islam and Christianity. The only religions that will be able to present themselves and to maintain their ground as 'world religions' in the future will be the ones that accept the 'single world' that is coming into being and the common world history which can be created today for the first time. This is the new situation for the religions, Christianity included.[2]

Historically, mission and the spread of Christianity created certain particular centres: the Roman empire, Europe and America. As a result a Christianity came into being which was centred on Rome; later this was followed by a Christianity centred on Europe and America. For a long time the Christian nations and states of Europe and America were the bulwark of Christianity against other nations and states, and also against other religions. In modern times, hand in hand with North Atlantic colonialism and imperialism, Christianity then spread all over the world. The other religions were either viewed as enemies or as the superstitions from which Christianity (in conjunction with Western civilization) freed men and women. This period of 'Western mission', with its opportunities and its burdens, is irrevocably coming to an end. The era of 'world mission' is beginning.[8] But what does this mean? Christianity is more or less present in all nations. But it is frequently only present in its Western form. Indigenous forms must therefore develop, so that an authentic Indian, Chinese, Japanese, Indonesian, African and Latin American Christianity may grow up, with corresponding indigenous theologies. The centring on Europe will come to an end. It further means that indigenous Christianity will enter into dialogue, exchange and mutual co-operation with the respective indigenous religions. In this way, without the support of Christian peoples and states, Christians will enter into living relationship with people of other faiths. The dialogue between powerless Christian minorities and the prevailing religions will look very different from the dialogue carried on by powerful Christian majorities. It will be pursued without the temptation to apply force. That is a new situation for the Christianity which is scattered all over the world.

What task can Christianity have towards the other world religions? It is one goal of mission to awaken faith, to baptize, to found churches and to form a new life under the lordship of Christ. Geographically this mission proceeds to the ends of the earth. It proceeds numerically and tries to reach as many people as possible. It thinks in terms of quantity and evolves strategies for 'church growth'. We have no intention of disputing this or belittling it. But mission has another goal as well. It lies in the qualitative alteration of life's atmosphere – of trust, feelings, thinking and acting. We might call this missionary aim to 'infect' people, whatever their religion, with the spirit of hope, love and responsibility for the world. Up to now this qualitative mission has taken place by the way and unconsciously, as it were, in the wake of the 'quantitative' mission. In the new world situation in which all religions find themselves, and the new situation of Christianity in particular, the qualitative mission directed towards an alteration of the whole atmosphere of life should be pursued consciously and responsibly. It will not be able to diffuse *en passant* the atmosphere of the Christian West, nor will it desire to do so. For this is neither particularly 'Christian' nor very helpful; and it is not what is wanted. But it will have to direct its energies towards the climate which is essential if solutions are to be found to the most serious problems which face mankind today – famine, domination of one class by another, ideological imperialism, atomic wars, and the destruction of the environment.

Qualitative mission takes place in dialogue. If it is a serious dialogue about the most fundamental problems, then it does not lead to non-commital permanent conversations. In dialogue the religions change, Christianity included, just as in personal conversations the expressions, attitudes and views of the partners alter. The dialogue of world religions is a process into which we can only enter if we make ourselves vulnerable in openness, and if we come away from the dialogue changed. We do not lose our identity, but we acquire a new profile in the confrontation with our partner. The world religions will emerge from the dialogues with a new profile. It may be said that Christians hope that these profiles will be turned towards suffering men and women and their future, towards life and towards peace.

If Christianity is to adapt itself to this process of dialogue, openness and alteration, a series of prejudices about other religions will have to be demolished.

THE ABSOLUTISM OF THE CHURCH

The Church's exclusive absolutism has made Christianity invulnerable, inalterable and aggressive. 'Outside the Church no salvation' was the definition of the Council of Florence in 1442, appealing to Cyprian and Origen. What it meant was:

> The Holy Roman Church . . . firmly believes, acknowledges and proclaims that 'no one outside the Catholic Church, neither heathen nor Jew nor unbeliever, nor anyone separated from the unity, will partake of eternal life, but that he will rather fall victim to the everlasting fire prepared for the devil and his angels, if he does not adhere to it [i.e. the Holy Roman Church] before he dies'.[4]

Here Jews, unbelievers and schismatics are lumped together into a group destined for mass perdition. The Roman Church is maintained as being the Church of salvation. It was at that time the imperial Church as well. The crusades, the Albigensian wars and the political persecutions of the groups mentioned were both the presupposition and the result of the declaration. It was not until five hundred years later that the Second Vatican Council amended the Catholic Church's attitude. Now 'all men of good will can achieve salvation', including Jews, Moslems and Christians belonging to other denominations, at least in principle.[5] For the whole group comprising all men 'of good will' (who are no more closely defined than that) is pronounced capable of salvation. This certainly opens the frontiers of the visible Church, defined by baptism and membership, and makes them more permeable; but the problem remains unsolved. A milder, opener, perhaps even 'more enlightened' absolutism takes the place of the old rigorous and violent one. But must the Church not rethink its position even more radically? Outside Christ no salvation.[6] Christ has come and was sacrificed for the reconciliation of the whole world. No one is excluded. Outside the salvation that Christ brings to all men there is therefore no Church. The visible Church is, as Christ's Church, the ministry of reconciliation exercised upon the world. Thus the Church is to be seen, not as absolute, but in its relationship to the divine reconciler and to reconciled men and women, of whatever religion.

THE ABSOLUTISM OF FAITH

The absolutism of faith with regard to the world religions also needs revision. Against the background of the modern criticism levelled at religion by Feuerbach, Marx, Freud and Nietzsche, the 'dialectical theologians' Karl Barth, Emil Brunner, Friedrich Gogarten and Rudolf Bultmann have emphatically shown that faith is not to be equated with religion. From the prophets and apostles onwards, the biblical faith itself has been conspicuously critical of religion. The enemies of faith are not lack of faith but superstition, idolatry, man's 'Godalmightiness' and self-righteousness. As the successor of the prophets, true faith acts iconoclastically against the idols and fetishes of timorous man. Following the crucified Christ, it acts irreligiously and 'atheistically' against the political religions and idols of countries and nations. Trust in the triune God strips away the aura of divinity from actualities that have been made into idols and makes life in the world in the framework of creation possible. Faith in 'the crucified God' robs power and fortune of the careless confidence from which they live and the superstitious fear which is the basis of their rule. Modern philosophical criticism o religion grew up from the religion of middle-class society. Feuerbach, Marx, Freud and Nietzsche understood relatively little about the world religions or the comparative study of religions. The criticism of religion levied by early dialectical theology had in view the relationship between faith and religion at a time when the bourgeois Christian world was declining. But it deepened the conflict of faith and religion theologically in such a way that man was presented with a general alternative: religion as the self-assertion of man, who feels himself lost – or faith as man's response to God's self-revelation? Its Christian criticism of religion was directed against the Christianity which has become 'religious' in this sense, not against the world religions. For that reason we cannot deduce the absolutism of Christianity over against the world religions from the theological difference between revelation and religion, faith and superstition. The relationship of Christianity to the other religions must be defined differently. The criticism of religion is directed on a quite different level to everyone, whether he be Christian, Jew, Moslem or Hindu. If we make a clear distinction here, we escape the absolute misunderstanding of the Christian faith on the one hand,

and avoid on the other the compulsion to set up a general concept of religion which levels down all religions, including Christianity.[7]

THE RELATIVISM OF THE ENLIGHTENMENT

The absolutism of the Church in Europe came to an end through the wars of religion and was replaced by the relativism of the Enlightenment and of humanism. People sought for the 'third way', the 'third era of the spirit' in the conflict between Catholics and Protestants. The more unknown continents were discovered, and the more strange religions became known, the more intensively people also looked for a general human basis in this whole field, in order to understand the things that were strange and to find peace. The tolerance of modern states towards Catholics and Protestants developed into a general tolerance towards the world religions. This tolerance, which was essential for peace, could be sustained for different reasons. It could be *sceptical tolerance*. If different groups claim absolute truth for very different things, then it would seem obvious to dispute such claims in general, and to hold anyone that maintains them for a charlatan. Sceptical tolerance is shown in the story of 'the three impostors' (Moses, Jesus and Mohammed are meant), which probably originated in the tenth century in the border region between Arabs and Christians. It has also been ascribed to the 'enlightened' Hohenstaufen emperor Frederick II. At all events this story acquired great influence during the period of the Enlightenment. But sceptical tolerance does not itself avoid the necessity of having to commit itself to the non-committal nature of all claims to truth. Lessing took up the story of the three impostors in his parable of the ring; but here *productive tolerance* replaces its sceptical counterpart:

> So let each man hold his ring
> To be the true one – even so
> Let each man press on uncorrupted
> After his love, free from all prejudice.

Lessing's productive tolerance did not criticize the different subjective modes of faith for their certainty, but he did criticize their dealings with one another. He wanted to see the dialogue of the world religions in history as a noble contest, in which every religion displays its best, without disparaging the others. For him history as a noble contest between the religions had as its goal the revelation of truth at the end of history. Because of that he relativized the religions in the light of this future, seeing them all side by side as forerunners of the future truth, which they only think they already possess. In the present he was able to discover the hidden future truth only in the ethos of humanity. The truth itself is 'undemonstrable'. It is only 'demonstrated' here and now through humanity. That is why Nathan says to the Sultan Saladin, after the parable of the ring, 'Ah, if I had but found one more among you for whom it sufficed to be a man!' For productive tolerance, every religion is a means of educating humanity and a transitional stage to pure morality. Lessing lived in a period of absolutist assertions of truth. 'Possession makes a man quiet, indolent and proud,' he remarks critically. His pointer to the hidden nature of truth seemed to mobilize man's best powers. If truth is 'undemonstrable', then continual striving after truth, even with the admitted risk of error, stands higher than its possession. Today, on the contrary, the hiddenness of truth does not seem to release any striving towards truth at all. The change from productive to sceptical tolerance dominates the secular age. The proposition that 'everyone should find salvation after his own fashion' had a meaning as long as people actually wanted salvation, and as long as one or another fashion of finding it presented itself. The relativity of 'the religions' which Lessing maintained in the face of the future manifestation of truth, and its relativity in view of humanity's present ethos, are perverted into their opposites when they turn into relativism. For religious, historical and moral relativism either has no basis at all, or it is based on another absolutism. Even today, if we would like to channel the world religions towards the essential peace of the world or the necessary classless society, so as to relativize their differences, we do not escape the mutual play of relativism and absolutism. For who has the right, or who is in a position, to set up the conditions and the goal which are to determine the ethos of the religions and their functions? Whose picture of humanity is to prevail and whose image of the goal is to dominate humanity's future? In most cases religious relativism seems simply to be a cloak for a new absolutism, even if it does not already behave absolutely itself. The truth of relativism and the tolerance founded on it is no doubt to be sought in relationality. A life and a religion are relative in that they behave relationally and enter into living relationships to other life and other religions. In living relationship 'everything' is not of equal consequence, and therefore of no consequence at all. The one is of extreme significance for the other. It is only out of the growing web of living relationships that something new can come into being for a wider community. Absolutism and relativism are really twins, because both view everything from a higher, non-historical watch-tower. In the open history of potentiality one can only move specifically from one relationship to other relationships in the hope that living relations will enable us to gain 'everything' and to combat the threat of 'nothingness'.

NATURE AND SUPERNATURE

At this point we may briefly consider the traditional theological models for the relationship between Christianity and the world religions. They start from Christianity in order to define the relationship according to Christian concepts; that is to say, they still belong to the period of Christian absolutism. 'Nature and supernature' was one model. According to this the other religions belong to the realm of nature, the natural knowledge of God and reverence for him. But the Christian Church lives from and represents a mystery which is known as 'supernatural'. It must therefore present itself as the supernatural truth of natural truths, or as the fullness of truth behind the elements of truth in the other religions. It is true that grace does not destroy nature, but rather completes it. But just for that very reason the Church must take up the other religions and perfect them in itself. Wherever the Church is implanted, therefore, it will take over all the elements which according to its supernatural wisdom, it holds to be 'good, true and beautiful', and will heighten them, correct them and so perfect them. We can find examples in the Christianization of Greek, Roman, Germanic and Latin-American religion. There was also a historical interpretation of the same model, according to which all the heathen religions are historically interim religions. Only Christianity can term itself 'the absolute religion' because it lives from the absolute self-manifestation of God and the eschatological presence of the Spirit. It contains within itself the completion of the history of divine Being and it represents the end of the history of religion. This model too allows for the integration of everything which is 'good, true and beautiful' in the provisional religions, measured by the yardstick of the absolute self-manifestation of God. It is also syncretistically open to the aspects of truth in other religions. But it is precisely because of its syncretistic openness that the Christian religion is to excel all others, so proving itself 'the absolute religion'.[8]

THE CRITICAL CATALYST

If Christianity renounces its exclusive claim in relation to the other religions, and if it does not assume an inclusive claim either, then the formula of the critical catalyst suggests itself as a new model for its post-absolutist era.[9] A catalyst causes elements to combine simply through its presence. The simple presence of Christians in environments determined by other religions provokes effects of this kind, provided that Christians live, think and act differently. This can be called the indirect infection of other religions with Christian ideas, values and principles. If it is true that the Indian religions think 'unhistorically', then their world picture is altered by the experience of reality as history which Christians present to them. This is already taking place through the historical investigation of Hinduism and Buddhism, through the introduction of, and stress on, the future tense in the Indian languages, and, finally, through the different relationship Christians have to time. If it is true that Islam produces a fatalistic attitude, then the encounter with Christianity brings about the discovery that the world can be changed and that people have a responsibility for changing it. If it is true that many religions have their faces so turned away from the world that they disseminate social indifference, then the presence of Christians makes them recognize social responsibility and the activities appropriate to it. But these indirect catalystic influences of Christianity on other religions are never unequivocal; they are always ambiguous, especially when they are linked with the spread of Western science and technology. Science and technology, capitalism or socialism, cannot be viewed as an indirect 'Christianization' of other religions. But these effects are there and must be noted. We must become conscious of them today so that the catalystic influences of the Christian faith can be less ambiguous than they have been, and are not confused with the influence of the West, merely under Christian auspices.

The models we have discussed are still not based on dialogue since they proceed from the Christian monologue, not from the dialogue itself. They all formulate the Christian position before the entry into dialogue. They do not formulate it in the context of dialogue. Consequently they still do not show any profile of Christianity in the context of dialogue. Christianity's vocation must be presented as clearly as possible, but it must be a presentation in relationship, and must not precede that relationship.

PROFILE IN THE CONTEXT OF DIALOGUE

The life in dialogue of the world religions is in its first modest and hesitant beginnings. It is therefore more important to formulate the first steps than to fix the comprehensive goals. Bilateral dialogues between Christians and Jews,

Christians and Moslems, Christians and Buddhists, Buddhists and Hindus, Moslems and animists, etc., can lead to multilateral dialogues; and multilateral dialogues can be the genesis of the tension-fraught universal community of religions for a universal society, though no one yet knows what it will look like.

We have talked about a qualitative mission, aimed at creating a climate for life in fellowship; and we have called its method dialogue. Out of bitter experience, the expression 'mission' has come to be taken as a threat by many people. Christians can only talk about their particular mission if they take note of and respect the different missions of other religions. They can only enter usefully into dialogue with them if they do not merely want to communicate something, but to receive something as well. Fruitful dialogue involves clear knowledge about the identity of one's own faith on the one hand; but on the other it requires a feeling of one's own incompleteness and a real sense of need for fellowship with the other. This is the only way in which real interest in another religion comes into being, a 'creative need for the other'.[10] The dialogue itself changes the atmosphere in which the religions formerly existed, separated from or even actively hostile to each other, and creates the conditions for fellowship in which mutual participation, exchange and cross-fertilization become possible.

The first experiences of dialogue of this kind led to a catalogue of the insights which other religions can pass on to Christianity.[11] The uniqueness of Islam's call 'Let God be God', its total recognition of the divine lordship over the whole of life, and its criticism of idolatry, both ancient and modern, must impress Christians and call them to self-examination. The meditative power of Buddhism, its insight into the self and man's inner freedom brings back to light repressed mystical elements in the Christian faith, and can lead Christians to re-examine their modern activism. Perception of the complicated systems of balance which bind together the individual, his community, the natural environment, his ancestors and the gods does not permit the prejudicial adjective 'primitive' to be applied to the animist religions of Africa and Asia. They probably preserve ecological and genetic knowledge which has long since been lost to modern Christianity.

The three-cornered dialogue between Jews, Christians and Moslems can fall back on common historical presuppositions and many existing parallels. The dialogue with Buddhists will first of all concentrate on the general human problem of suffering. Conversations with the popular religions can, in the first place, revolve round 'the feast'. There are starting points enough, once interest has been awakened. But we shall only be able to discover what they are through dialogue. Here the level of the dialogue will first have to be found in each individual relationship. It is not possible to determine this level from the Christian side by means of theological scholarship; for 'theology' is a Christian speciality and peculiarity, and theology as a discipline has only existed in Christianity since the Middle Ages. Other religions have other forms of expression, and so will wish to choose their own level of dialogue, e.g. the cult, meditation, or other areas of religious practice. For this reason Christians cannot determine in advance that the relationship is to be one of dialogue on an intellectual level. But, like every other religion, Christianity must none the less be clear about what it hopes for when it enters into living relationships and into dialogue with others. And here the dialogue cannot be the means to an unspoken end; how far the dialogue itself is hope is something that must be clarified.

'Dialogue strives to bring to expression the love which alone makes truth creative.'[12] For Christianity dialogue and the relationships to other religions are not a means to an end; they are meaningful in themselves as an expression of its life in love. For it lives in the presence of a God who is love and who desires love. It lives in a God who can suffer and who in the power of his love desires to suffer in order to redeem. In their dialogue with people of a different faith, Christians cannot therefore testify through their behaviour to an unalterable, apathetic and aggressive God. By giving love and showing interest in others, they also become receptive to the other and vulnerable through what is alien to them. They can bear the otherness of the others without becoming insecure and hardening their hearts. The right thing is not to carry on the dialogue according to superficial rules of communication, but to enter into it out of the depths of the understanding of God. In that way we testify to God's openness to men in our openness to other people and other things. In that way we show God's passion through our living interest in the other. In that way we manifest God's vulnerability in the vulnerability of our love and our readiness for change. To isolate oneself and to seek to dominate even in mission are probably always signs of incapacity to suffer. The God who wins power in the world through the helplessness of his Son, who liberates through his self-giving, and whose strength is mighty in weakness can only be testified to in dialogue and in the wounds and transformations which dialogue brings with it.

It was said to be one of the highlights of the ecumenical dialogue when a Shiite Moslem, with his tradition of the sovereign God, felt the lack of God's self-surrender to man, the God who suffers and sacrifices himself.[13] This must not be overvalued, or stressed as a missionary success, but it can be interpreted as an indication that human suffering is the central problem in most religions. Is it solved when the Buddhist tries to extinguish the 'desire' of life as the ground of suffering? Is it solved if the animist sees it as a disturbance in the cosmic balance and tries to put the disturbance right through sacrifice? Is it solved when the Moslem accepts his destiny in total self-surrender to God? Is it solved if the Christian accepts suffering in the love of God and transforms it by virtue of his hope? Dialogue is not merely a way of discussing suffering; it is also a way of practising our attitudes to suffering on one another.

This complex of dialogue, vulnerability and the question of suffering leads to the step beyond inter-religious dialogue, to the human situation today. The fellowship in dialogue of the religions would be misunderstood if it went under the slogan: religions of the world unite against growing irreligious secularism or antireligious Communism! On the contrary, inter-religious dialogue must be expanded by dialogue with the ideologies of the contemporary world. Together with them, it must ultimately be related to the people who are living, suffering and dying in the world today.

When we consider the indigenization of the Christian churches and Christian theology in any given society, this orientation also raises the question of the place of their presence in the social structure. In societies which are divided up into castes and classes, it matters very much whether the Christian churches and theology make themselves at home in the ruling castes or classes, in the lower castes or classes, or among the casteless and classless. Historically, too, it made a difference whether Christianity spread through the conversion and baptism of kings, or through the conversion and liberation of the poor. It is true that today national and social identity often overlap.

But just because of that the national and cultural indigenization of Christianity is by no means sufficient. It must also come to be at home among the people; and what will be at home among them is whatever shares their necessities and works for their liberation.

This orientation towards the suffering of the present time also raises questions about the social position of the partners in the dialogue between world religions. Top-level discussions between privileged persons usually do very little to relieve the suffering of ordinary people. Dialogue is a sign of hope for these people if it is carried on in the interests of their life and liberation. In the interests of cultural indigenization, a truly Indian, Chinese, Japanese, Indonesian, Arabic and African Christianity must come into being. Moreover, in the dialogue with the world religions a Buddhist, Hindu, Moslem, animist, Confucian, Shintoist Christianity will come into being. There were Jewish reasons for believing Jesus to be the Christ. There were Greek reasons for believing in Jesus as the Logos. There were Germanic reasons for reverencing Jesus as the leader of souls. In their own period these reasons were not merely cultural; they were more religious in kind. Culture and religion cannot be separated. Consequently, today we shall also have to enquire into Hindu, Buddhist and Islamic reasons for faith in Jesus. This must not be condemned as syncretism. A Christianity coloured by different civilizations does not result in a cultural mixture; and a Christianity tinged with different religions does not simply produce a religious mixture. What is at issue is the charismatic quickening of different religious gifts, powers and potentialities for the kingdom of God and the liberation of men. The syncretism which dissolves Christian identity only comes about if people lose sight of this future, to which Christianity is called. Mere indigenization in another culture and religion looks back to what has come into existence and to what is actually present. The charismatic activation of cultural and religious forces in the interests of the messianic future looks forward. If it is Christianity's particular vocation to prepare the messianic era among the nations and to make ready the way for the coming redemption, then no culture must be pushed out and no religion extinguished. On the contrary, all of them can be charismatically absorbed and changed in the power of the Spirit. They will not be ecclesiasticized in the process, nor will they be Christianized either; but they will be given a messianic direction towards the kingdom. For this, people of other religions, and the other religions themselves, bring a wealth of potentialities and powers with them; and Christianity must not suppress these but must fill them with hope. Then the dialogue of world religions can also become a sign of hope for the people who have no definite religion or religious practice, but whose elemental cry is for liberation, life and redemption. For Christianity the dialogue with the world religions is part of the wider framework of the liberation of the whole creation for the coming kingdom. It belongs within the same context as the conversation with Israel and the political and social passion for a freer, juster and more habitable world. Christianity's dialogistic profile ought to be turned to the future of the liberating and redeeming kingdom in the potentialities and powers of the world religions. That is a profile which Christianity can only acquire in dialogue with others.

1. In this paragraph I have drawn particularly on *Living Faiths and the Ecumenical Movement*, ed. S. J. Samartha, World Council of Churches, Geneva, 1971.
2. Cf. the four volumes published in preparation for the Geneva Conference on Church and Society: *Christian*

Social Ethics in a Changing World, ed. J. C. Bennett; *Responsible Government in a Revolutionary Age*, ed. Z. K. Matthews; *Economic Growth in World Perspective*, ed. D. Munby; and *Man in Community*, ed. E. de Vries, all SCM Press and Association Press 1966. See also J. Moltmann, 'Bringing Peace to a Divided World', *The Experiment Hope*, ET SCM Press and Fortress Press, 1975, pp. 72ff.

3. At the Bangkok Conference in 1973 this new situation was both demanded and evident. See *Bangkok Assembly 1973*, Minutes and Report of the Assembly . . . on World Mission and Evangelism, Geneva, 1973.
4. Quoted from H. Küng, *On Being a Christian*, p. 97. I agree with his criticism of this theological formula.
5. K. Rahner expressly supported this ecclesiological expansion of the concept of the Church: see 'Anonymous Christians', *Theological Investigations* VI, ET Darton, Longman & Todd and Seabury Press, 1969, pp. 390ff. Here, unlike Rahner, we are adhering to the integration of the concept of the Church in 'God's history' with the world, which we have already discussed.
6. So H. Küng, *Christenheit als Minderheit*, Einsiedeln, 1965, p. 36: 'We can ask what is outside the Church, but the question is difficult to answer. But what is outside God and his plan of salvation is no question at all. If we look at God's plan of salvation, then there is no *extra*, only an *intra*, no outside, only an inside, since God "desires all men to be saved and to come to the knowledge of the truth. For there is one God, and there is one mediator between God and men, the man Christ Jesus, who gave himself as a ransom for *all*" [1 Timothy 2:5f.].'
7. H. Küng links his criticism of my book *The Crucified God* in his essay 'Die Religionen als Frage an die Theologie des Kreuzes' (*EvTh* 33, 1973, pp. 401–23) with a recollection of early dialectical theology and its neglect of the question of the world religions. His essay is not designed 'to set up a counter-position to the theology of the cross but to give the necessary (Catholic) way of access to a theology which is rightly based on the Gospel' (p. 404). In *On Being A Christian* Küng put the question, 'Superior ignorance?', to

the dialectical theologians. I hope I may be able to convince him that we are working together for an 'open theology of the cross' (p 420). The more central the cross becomes, the more open the interest in other religions and the richer and broader the pneumatology. But this is really as much as to say: the more 'Evangelical' the more 'Catholic'!

8. This argument was put forward by W. Pannenberg, 'Towards a Theology of the History of Religions', *Basic Questions in Theology* II, ET SCM Press and Fortress Press, 1971, pp. 65ff. F. Wagner, *Uber die Legitimät der Mission*, *ThEx* 154, Munich, 1968, pp. 45f., has taken these ideas further in his own way in order to prove Christianity's ancient 'claim to absoluteness' through its syncretistic openness for 'the elements of truth in other religions'.
9. Cf. H. Küng, *On Being A Christian*, pp. 110ff.: 'Christian existence as critical catalyst'.
10. *Living Faiths and the Ecumenical Movement*, p. 18.
11. Compare here the values other religions can contribute to Christianity which are named in *Living Faiths and the Ecumenical Movement* (passim) with Küng's list of the values Christianity can contribute to other religions (*On Being A Christian*, pp. 104ff.). Christians ought to begin with the values of the other religions. The representatives of other religions should talk about Christian values. Küng observes: 'For historical reasons, Western science and technology contain far too many elements stemming from the Jewish-Christian tradition for it to be easy to take over Western science and technology without calling one's own religious position in question' (p. 111). The observation can easily be misunderstood in an apologetic sense. Christianity itself is very much called in question by 'Western science and technology', in spite of the allegedly 'far too many elements' in them deriving from Jewish-Christian tradition.
12. *Living Faiths and the Ecumenical Movement*, p. 34.
13. *Ibid.*, p. 92.

11. THE THEOLOGICAL BASIS OF INTERFAITH DIALOGUE

John V. Taylor

I feel deeply both the honour and the responsibility of being called to give this lecture in these historic and august surroundings [the first Lambeth Interfaith Lecture, November 1977]. I feel also a keen sense of regret that what I have to say – and I mean, what I *have* to say from inner conviction and compulsion – is probably going to disappoint those of my audience who with an equal conviction which I respect believe that the way to mutual understanding and reconciliation between the great faiths of mankind is already open and clear and needs only a willingness to follow it. I don't believe we are yet in sight of any such way, and my address therefore is a plea for patience and persistence in dialogue. And dialogue, as I understand it, means a sustained conversation between parties who are not saying the same thing and who recognize and respect the differences, the contradictions, and the mutual exclusions, between their various ways of thinking. The object of this dialogue is understanding and appreciation, leading to further reflection upon the implication for one's own position of the convictions and sensitivities of the other traditions.

APPRECIATION MUST PRECEDE RECONCILIATION OF IDEAS

This is a more exacting exercise than any of us would wish

for, because every human being finds it difficult to sustain contradictions and live with them. Instinctively we either try to destroy what is opposed to our understanding of truth or we pretend that the antithesis is unreal. The reason for this is, I believe, that we are all naturally frightened by the unresolved opposites in ourselves and find it very painful to include and accept the dark self alongside the light, the destroyer as well as the creator in us, both the male and the female element in our personality, both the child and the parent which we are. We want to be a simple unity but in fact we are a structure of contradictions. It takes a high degree of maturity to let the opposites co-exist without pretending that they can be made compatible. It takes the same maturity to respect an opinion that conflicts with one's own without itching to bring about a premature and naïve accommodation. I suppose this is what is entailed in loving one's enemies. One has to appreciate the reason for their opposition, grant its integrity, and deal honestly with its challenges, without surrendering any of one's own integrity or diminishing the content of one's examined convictions. And there will generally have to be a great deal of that kind of loving before we can expect any genuine reconciliation of ideas and beliefs. The loving which is expressed through the attempt to listen and understand and honour, through the frank recognition and appreciation of convictions that deny one's own, through the opening of one's imagination to the real otherness of the other, is, in my view, the function of interfaith dialogue.

PAST ISOLATION HAS BRED IGNORANCE AND SUSPICION

We have a lot of leeway to make up, for we have all suffered from hundreds of years of religious isolation. During the first few centuries of the Church's history Christians took it as a matter of course that they were surrounded by people with different religions from their own. They had to face questions about their own practice and belief posed by their Jewish environment first of all and, soon after, by the Graeco-Roman culture or the religions of Parthia and further east. They had to learn how to keep themselves separate for survival, but they also had to learn how to reconcile their undeniable spiritual experience with the framework of ideas that supported these other faiths and philosophies. Religious pluralism was the milieu of the first Christians.

But the society of Western Christendom, in which the thought and tradition of our Church was developed and fixed, was very different. It was hemmed in by the encircling power and superior culture of Islam and confined to the western corner of the vast Euro-Asian continent. Had the Church of those centuries been so minded it might have developed a positive and open relationship with the Jewish communities in its midst. Unhappily this was not its mood and, in any case, the greatest flowering of Jewish culture and teaching took place in Islamic Spain, cut off from contact with Christendom.

As a counter aggression the Church developed a crusading ethos that became a fundamental feature of its tradition, an ethos which even today is second nature to many Christians. That stirring poem of heroic war, the

Song of Roland, reflects the utter ignorance of Islam which was typical of Christian thought in the eleventh century. Muslims are regarded as pagans and polytheists, worshipping three great idols called Mahmoud, Termagent and Apolyon! My guess is, though I do not have access to the evidence, that the popular notions of Christianity among Muslims or even Jews of those days were equally ignorant. In the case of Islam, indeed, some of the misconceptions are actually enshrined in the Holy Qu'ran, and thereby given an even greater immutability.

One of the bitter fruits of this long history of non-communication is the tendency in every religious culture to read deliberate hostility into the quite innocent attitudes of people of another faith. I recall a fairly typical experience at Rawalpindi in 1968 when I was invited to meet the staff of the Islamic Research Institute. A very liberal and remarkably open discussion was traumatically upset by the intervention of a young historian from North Africa who protested that the contemporary Church was as relentlessly hostile to Islam as it had ever been, and he instanced missionary sympathy with the Southern Sudanese revolt, widespread Christian rejoicing over Israel's capture of the Old City of Jerusalem, and the churches' support of Biafra. I would place in the same category the widespread Jewish conviction that the hesitancy of Christian leaders to endorse every advance of the Jewish State is evidence of their immutable antagonism, and the tendency of many African Christians to see behind the atrocities of Amin a pan-Islamic policy of expansion. Dialogue, as I understand it, means overcoming the immediate urge to dismiss these suspicions as untrue, accepting the fact that, true or not, the suspicions are part of the data of our relationships, and facing the possibility that perhaps the other person has more reason to be suspicious of me than I have hitherto admitted. If we all made that effort of imagination it might make us humbler and gentler.

EACH RELIGION IS A TRADITION OF RESPONSE BY ORDINARY PEOPLE

We come to the dialogue, therefore, lumbered with our past histories and the fears they have engendered in us. But if we are to go forward history must be forgotten, or at least forgiven. For dialogue is between the living, the people of here and now. Dialogue seeks a new beginning. Dialogue also has to take account mainly of the normal adherents of the different faiths, not the great saints nor the great sinners, for in a sense they prove very little. I was reminded of this a month ago in Assisi where two Franciscan stories were retold to me one after the other. The first concerns Saint Francis's strange meeting with Sala'din. They had no common language, so little dialogue can have taken place. Yet near the end of the encounter Sala'din is reported to have said, 'If ever I met a second Christian like you I would be willing to be baptized. But that will not happen.' And less than 300 years later a King in Peru said something very similar, yet horribly different, to a Franciscan friar. This friar, accompanying an expedition of the Conquistadores, was offering the vanquished Incas the choice of conversion or death. When their King demurred, his hands were cut off and the appeal was then repeated: 'Be baptized and you will go to heaven.' 'No,' said the King, 'for if I went to heaven I might meet a second Christian like you.' Those two incidents may show the terrible liability to decline which is inherent in any great spiritual movement. But they also warn us against focusing our dialogue upon the exceptionally good or bad in the history of any religion.

For I believe we should think of every religion as a people's particular tradition of response to the reality which the Holy Spirit of God has set before their eyes. I am deliberately not saying that any religion is the truth which the Spirit has disclosed, nor even that it contains that truth. I think it may often be misleading to speak of the various religions as revelations of God, for that suggests that God has disclosed part of himself to one people and a different part to others. Is that how a compassionate father loves the various children of his family? It is surely truer to believe that God's self-revelation and self-giving is consistent for all, but that different peoples have responded differently. All we can say without presumption is that that is how men in a particular culture have responded and taught others to respond to what the Spirit of God through the events of their history and the vision of their prophets made them aware of. By putting it this way we do justice both to the God-given element and to the manmade element in every religion. We also leave room for the recognition that every religious tradition includes the response of disobedience as well as the response of obedience. For human beings can use religion against God or as an escape from him just as much as they use religion for God and as an approach to him. And both the obedience and the disobedience get built into the tradition and passed on to later generations. And they, in their turn, may respond more readily to the unceasing calls and disclosures of the Spirit, and so be moved to reform some part of the tradition. So every living faith is found to be in a continual process of renewal and purification while at the same time it conserves the tradition and transmits it as something recognizably the same. In every religion, therefore, we shall find the same tension between conservatism and development, and it must be so if past fidelity and present response are both to be seen as an answer to Him who is beyond all religion.

But since every religion is a historically determined tradition of response to what the Spirit of God has forever been setting before men's eyes, we must expect to find that each religion has become a self-consistent and almost closed system of culture and language. Communication between one such system and another is fraught with difficulty which must not be underestimated. As dialogue begins, therefore, we shall frequently find that the same word carries an entirely different cluster of meanings in the different traditions; we may also discover with surprise that quite different words are used to mean the same thing. I recall a very well-known and respected participant in the dialogue between Christians and Hindus exclaiming in the course of a conversation – 'What makes this so painful is that again and again, when my Hindu brother and I seem to be drawing closer than ever before, and at a deeper level, at that very moment the immense gulf between us opens up again.'

This is to a considerable extent a problem of hermeneutics, the structure of meanings in communication. Different cultures develop different horizons of understanding, as they are called. And therein lies some degree of hopefulness. Professor Heinrich Ott of Basle University, speaking at the World Council of Churches consultation at Chiang Mai in Thailand in April, said: 'We can look for a partial convergence of the horizons of understanding on the two sides. There arises a new common horizon for the partners in the dialogue, a new world, so to speak, with new possibilities and understanding and speech – and therefore the disclosure of new theological dimensions.'

JOHN V. TAYLOR

THE OPEN, INCLUSIVE VIEW IN CHRISTIAN THEOLOGY

Christians ought not to imagine that there is anything particularly new or radical in this open attitude to the other great faiths. In spite of the long isolation of the Middle Ages and the theology of exclusive salvation which is familiar to us, there has always been in the Jewish-Christian tradition another more inclusive view of the wideness of God's grace and redemption.

The exclusive covenant with Israel is not the only one in the Old Testament. The covenant with Noah embracing all the sons of men and, indeed, all creation, reverberates through the words of much later prophets and psalmists. God has shown his particular favour in more than one exodus deliverance. 'Have I not brought up Israel out of the land of Egypt, and the Philistines from Caphtor, and the Syrians from Kir?' (Amos 9:7). More than one nation, therefore, enjoys the experience of being chosen for blessing and for bringing blessing to the world. 'In that day shall Israel be the third with Egypt and Assyria, a blessing in the midst of the earth: for the Lord of Hosts has blessed them, saying: Blessed be Egypt my people, and Assyria the work of my hands, and Israel mine inheritance' (Isaiah 19:25). Therefore any sense of exclusive privilege on the part of a particular religion, including the Church, lays it open to a stringent judgement in comparison to the other faiths of men. 'From the rising of the sun to the going down of the same my name is great among the Gentiles, and in every place incense is offered in my name and a pure offering. But you have profaned it' (Malachi 1:11). Does it not seem likely that this haunting reference to the rising and going down of the sun was in the mind of Jesus when he pointed to the faith of the Roman centurion, saying: 'Many shall come from the East and from the West and shall sit down with Abraham and Isaac and Jacob in the Kingdom of heaven, but the sons of the Kingdom shall be cast into outer darkness' (Matthew 8:11f.). The Church cannot read those words today without applying them to itself, and, indeed, they strike at the heart of all exclusive religious claims.

Following up this element in the Gospel, Paul also refers more than once to God's universal disclosure of himself, and this is not only in the book of the Acts but in the Epistles as well. 'For all that may be known of God by men lies plain before their eyes, indeed God has disclosed it to them himself' (Romans 1:19). He goes on, of course, to show how universally men have closed their eyes against the truth made known to them, but that is a theme I have already touched upon in calling religions 'traditions of response'. When we examine the later teaching of the Church we find that the stark statement, 'No salvation outside the Church', was never allowed to go unmodified. Justin Martyr, for example, wrote: 'Christ is the firstborn of God and we have declared that he is the Word of whom every race of men were partakers; and those who lived according to the Logos are Christians even though they have been thought atheists, as, among the Greeks, Socrates and Heraclitus.' And Augustine, writing as an old man in his *Retractions*, made this startling statement: 'The reality itself, which we now call the Christian religion, was present among the early people, and up to the time of the coming of Christ was never absent from the beginning of the human race: so that the true religions which already existed now began to be called Christian.' I am very sensitive of the arrogance that such a statement must seem to convey to adherents of other great faiths today, and I shall deal with that problem in a moment. At this point my concern is to show the presence of an inclusive as well as an exclusive theology of the world religions in the Christian tradition.

But what about Saint Peter's often quoted and clear claim that 'there is no other name given among men by which we may be saved'? Wait a minute. What was the context of that affirmation? He was referring to the cure of the crippled beggar at the Beautiful Gate of the Temple. He was saying that Jesus of Nazareth is the source of every act of healing and salvation that has ever happened. He knew perfectly well that vast numbers of people had been healed without any knowledge of this Jesus, yet he made the astounding claim that Jesus was the hidden author of all healing. He was the totally unique saviour because he was totally universal.

Now I am not addicted to proof-texts, and if I were I would be beset by a species of gadfly that attacks all teachers of Christianity in these days, insisting that any text that seems to prove something is *ipso facto* suspect. But even if Peter did not make quite such a categorical or far-reaching assertion, it is clear that almost from the start Christians have claimed some kind of identity between Jesus of Nazareth and the life-giving forces of the creation, between the historic man and the universal principle. Jesus, they say, is central to what St Paul called 'the predeterminate purpose of God'.

CHRISTIANS CLAIM AN ABSOLUTE CENTRALITY FOR JESUS CHRIST

We should remember, in passing, that this kind of claim is not peculiar to the Christian religion. The Muslim would say, I believe, that the Holy Qu'ran is central to the predeterminate purpose of God. For the Jew, God's covenant with Israel and her settlement in the Holy Land is central to the divine purpose for all mankind. For the Buddhist the concept of the Buddha in one form or another is central to the purpose behind human existence. It is the nature of religious experience to put into the believer's hands a key which is absolute and irreducible. But when one considers the different things that are claimed as the key, comparisons crumble.

For the Christian, this belief that Jesus is central to God's purpose for mankind ought logically to relieve him of anxiety and argument about the salvation and future destiny of those whose lives are lived out within other traditions of response. This should not be the major issue in our theological reflection about the significance of the world religions. The phrase 'before the foundation of the world' occurs in two significant New Testament texts: the well-known verse in Revelation that describes the Lamb slain before the foundation of the world, and Ephesians 1:4 which says that 'in Christ he chose us before the world was founded'. Both texts tell us something about the constitution of the universe we inhabit. Both texts employ a startling metaphor of a time before time began. If we first accept his metaphor or image without unravelling it into non-mythical terms, it says that from the beginning the world was held in existence by the Redeemer who was to die. This is a pre-forgiven universe. God had chosen in eternity to take upon himself the risk and the cost of creating this kind of world. As a precondition of creation he took upon himself the judgement and death of the sinner. Being forgiven is therefore a more primary condition of man than being a sinner. Being in Christ is a more essential human state than being in ignorance of

Christ. So any and every movement of man's mind and will that can properly be called a response of faith is truly faith in Christ to some degree even though Christ is still only the invisible magnetic pole that draws us on.

But perhaps it makes more sense to our modern minds if we unravel this time metaphor. Its meaning must have something to do with the connection between God's being and God's doing – what God is eternally in himself, and what God does, which is necessarily within time. Now the peculiar insight of the Bible, which has recently been strongly endorsed by at least one school of Western philosophy, is this: There is no such thing as merely being, not even in God. One *is* only what one has done, or what one is inwardly and irrevocably committed to doing. This concept often eludes us because of the influence of Greek abstraction upon our thought. To say that a person is loving or just is actually meaningless until that person is committed in particular acts of love and justice. It is by acting truly and consistently at moments when the opposite is a real alternative that one comes to be truthful and reliable. Action creates being – not the other way round. No person and not even God can be merciful and forgiving in the abstract or in a timeless vacuum where there is nothing and no one to forgive. So we might truly say that in order to be the Father whose property it is always to have mercy it is necessary for God to have committed himself to a concrete act of bearing the death of the sinner. This is not to say that God's existence is contingent on the events of history. He is contingent only upon his own sovereign commitment *to be what he will be.* But that itself is a commitment to action in time. So, with our minds open to recognize the reality of the experience of divine grace and salvation within all the faiths of mankind, we can say that what God did through Jesus Christ is the one act which it was always necessary that he should accomplish in time and at the right time if he was to be the God who throughout time is accessible and present to every human being in judgement and mercy, grace and truth. Or, in other words, wherever we see people enjoying a living relationship with God and experiencing his grace we are seeing the fruits of Calvary though this may neither be acknowledged nor known. It still makes a vast difference to people when they have seen the Cross of Jesus as the indicator of the inner nature of God, and that remains the theme of the Christian witness. But in bearing that witness we do not have to deny the reality of the experiences of grace and salvation that are found, because of Christ, in all the faiths of mankind.

EVERY RELIGION HAS ITS 'JEALOUSIES'

You will realize, of course, that in what I have just said I have been talking as a Christian to Christians and wrestling with a theological problem in Christian terms. I recognize that the claims I have made for the person of Jesus are quite unacceptable to friends whose religion is different from mine. Yet I profoundly believe that this *kind* of statement should be welcomed from any of the parties in interfaith dialogue. It is not enough to limit our search to the areas of common ground, though these will always give us deep satisfaction when we find them. For there is something else which is in fact common to us all and that is what I would call the 'jealousies' of the different faiths. I mean those points in every religion concerning which the believers are inwardly compelled to claim a universal significance and finality. I have already referred to some of them – the Muslim conviction that the Holy

Qu'ran is not just another revelation but is God's last word; the Jewish conviction that Israel's covenant and her attachment to the Holy Land has a central significance in the determinate purpose of God; the Christian conviction that in the life and death and resurrection of Jesus God acted decisively for all mankind. The great faiths of Southern Asia may be inclined to argue that such absolute claims are typical of the semitic religions only; yet after many conversations I begin to wonder whether Hindu relativism is not itself another of those absolutes of a particular faith which cannot be surrendered without destroying the essential identity of that faith. All such convictions are strictly irreducible. I call them the 'jealousies' of the different faiths, deliberately using that ambiguous word, because seen from outside a particular household of faith such claims are bound to seem narrowly possessive; but within the household they reflect an experience which cannot be gainsaid. Every profoundly convincing encounter with God is with a jealous God. This simply means that having experienced God in that way, no other God will do. It is totally unhelpful to condemn such responses as arrogant. The meaning of things conveyed by such an experience is of such moment that it must be seen to have universal relevance, and to deny this is to be false to the experience itself.

So my Muslim brother says, 'Every child is born a Muslim', and I know what he means precisely because I have to say, 'Every child is born in Christ'. It is too facile to say simply that we mean the same thing. Each of us can recognize the contradiction between our views. But, given a deep mutual respect for one another's irreducible conviction, this does not bring our discourse to a standstill. As Professor Heinrich Ott put it during the World Council of Churches' Consultation at Chiang Mai, 'Genuine dialogue will not then be prevented by the belief of each partner that the ultimate and deepest insight into the truth nevertheless lies on his side.' Nor, I would add, will it be prevented by the longing in each of the participants that the other shall come in his own way to see the truth of that insight. If we sustain our dialogue undaunted by the emergence of these rock-like contradictions and exclusions we shall, in fact, find what Father Yves Raguin of the Society of Jesus called at that same consultation 'the paradox that there is no dialogue possible unless we realize the magnitude of the differences and try *from this* to find a common ground'. In other words, one of the most significant things we have in common on which to build our mutual understanding is the experience of having a conviction that by definition precludes the other person's belief, and of being unable to accommodate it with integrity. One recalls the underlying truth of Kipling's hackneyed verse:

> Oh, East is East and West is West, and never the
> twain shall meet,
> Till Earth and Sky stand presently at God's great
> judgement seat;
> But there is neither East nor West, Border nor
> Breed nor Birth,
> When two strong men stand face to face,
> though they come from the ends of the earth.

So I would again plead with those who want to make all the intractable convictions relative and level them down for the sake of a quick reconciliation: leave us at least our capacity for categorical assertion, for that is what we have in common.

So let us not deceive one another about these absolute

claims. They cannot be relativized, and the idea that the great faiths can be harmonized by doing that is too shallow. In our discourse with adherents of other faiths we may put our particular 'jealousies' in parenthesis, as it were, and have our private reservations, but we must not expect one another to abandon them. We may learn to reformulate these irreducible convictions in the light of our dialogue. But we know that the reformulation may never reduce or dilute the content of the experience which it interprets.

SOME EXPERIENCES HAVE TO BE ABSOLUTE AND UNIVERSALIZED

Let me explain that with reference again to the Christian position. I take an example that is currently in the fore-front of our Christian debate, the doctrine of the Incar-nation. We need to distinguish three stages of development:

(*a*) The impact which Jesus of Nazareth made upon those who knew him and those who heard about him which compelled them to make extraordinary claims about his authority and his identity;
(*b*) The resurrection experience which vindicated and enlarged those claims;
(*c*) The Church's recognition of the implications of these claims and her attempts to fit them into the ideas about God which already existed.

It seems pretty clear that the question, 'Whom do ye say that I am?' was not only put into the mouth of Jesus by the later teachers of the Christian Church, but was thrust upon people during the ministry of Jesus of Nazareth by the authority of his words and actions and personality.

Even before the resurrection, certain titles were being given to him, though we may argue whether they originated in his own thought or in his followers' response to him. But in whatever way we argue these points, we must hold to the fact that the Christian belief in the divinity of Jesus grew out of the overwhelming impact which he made upon people then, and still continues to make. What makes the first apostolic witnesses so remarkable is that, as they thought out the implications of the response they had been compelled to make to Jesus, they refused to retract any part of that response or diminish the claims they were making for him, even when it began to appear that their response and their claims were in conflict with all the accepted ideas about God. The first Christians were astonishingly fearless in pursuing the implications of the response to him which Jesus had compelled. It was not a case of gathering new ideas from the mystery religions or from Greek philosophy, nor even from the Old Testament, and building them into a theology about Jesus which moved beyond the original experience. On the contrary, what we see during the first four centuries of the Christian Church is a logical following-out of the implications of an original experience which they were not prepared to deny. One might say that they were according Jesus the lordship of their universe long before they dared to say, in so many words, that he was their *Kurios.* They were worshipping God in him long before they ventured to speak of his divinity. They had been saved by him long before they had worked out any theory of salvation. And what we see in St Paul, and in all the later Christian teachers, is a bold experimenting with one metaphor after another to describe their experience and fit it into their understanding of God and the universe. If the theologians of the early centuries failed – and I think we have to admit that in some of their formulations they did fail – it was because they stuck too rigidly to their previous ideas about God which owed more to a philosophical system than to a living experience. Through most of its history, the Church has gone on trying to maintain belief in the God who can undergo neither change nor suffering; yet, for those who have seen the glory of God in the face of Jesus Christ, that old axiom has had to be abandoned. What we say about Jesus Christ is that, if our idea of God differs in any respect from what we see in him and in his life, death and resurrection, then it is our idea of God that has to be changed; and not because of any prescribed dogma, but because, once we have seen him, we could not find it in us to worship a God who was different. Or, as someone has recently said, the impact of Jesus is such that, thereafter, only a wounded God will do.

WE MUST EXPOSE OUR EXPERIENCE TO ONE ANOTHER'S QUESTIONING

I have again been talking as a Christian to Christians, aware that others have been overhearing our debate on a central theme of our faith. But I make no apology for that because I believe that, if interfaith dialogue is to become sincere and deep, we have got to expose to one another the ways in which, within our separate households of faith, we wrestle with the questions that other religions put to us. To be overheard as we face up to these disconcerting questions will make us very vulnerable to one another. But if we are not ready to lower our defences, if in fact we are more interested in scoring points than in knowing one another, we may as well give up dialogue altogether.

So, besides letting one another know the absolutes in their own faith that may not be surrendered, the partners in the dialogue must also give serious reflection to the critique which each inevitably brings to bear upon the convictions of the others, however painful and disturbing this may be. If, as I have said, our irreducible loyalties belong to our experiences, and only secondarily to the doctrines that enshrine them, then we must be prepared to have the experiences questioned. Christians, for example, must allow their discourse with Jews to re-open a question which has troubled us from the earliest days: How can Jesus be Messiah and agent of the eschatological Kingdom, when it is so patent that things are not made new and the End is still awaited? Defensiveness ought not to make us unwilling to admit that this constitutes a real problem for us. Jewish experience through history may have a lot of light to throw upon the mystery of non-fulfilment in the covenants of God, and the hiddenness of God's victories. The Jewish-Christian dialogue, if pursued with mutual compassion, might blossom into a new theological understanding of the meaning of hope.

Or, again, the questions that Hinduism asks about the true definition of Christ's relation to God – asked in unaffected concern as often as in dispute – should send the Christians back not to abandon their claims but to a fresh exploration of terms and metaphors, just as the challenge of Greek philosophy did in the early centuries. After some years of intensive dialogue with Hindu friends, Klaus Klostermeier wrote: 'It will never be possible to contain Christ's mystery and the essence of Christianity completely and adequately in terms and ideas . . . If we start to ponder over the terms used by Greek christologists and think them out to their logical extremes, then we fall into absurdities and heresies. The first christologists were so aware of the newness of Christ and of the inadequacy of all known terms, that they preferred to talk about Christ paradoxically . . . A seeming contradiction, it is, however, the only means that compels our thinking to excel itself . . . Christ is neither the incarnation of the Jewish idea of God nor the apotheosis of the Greek idea of man. In India, too, we will have to make use of paradoxes, in order to lay open the mystery of Christ: the paradox evokes an existential cognition because it compels man to surpass the purely terminological, to advance into the essence, into the one reality where no contradiction subsists.'

To reformulate involves risking the loss of the original truth, yet it is also the only way in which that truth can live and grow into fuller comprehension. Reappraisal of one's own tradition and reformulation of one's own fidelities calls for an extraordinary mixture of humility and boldness. I have to put the question: Do all the partners in the interfaith dialogue come with an equal degree of self-questioning? I sometimes wonder, from what I have seen, whether Christians, for all our past aggressiveness, are not now exhibiting a greater share of self-criticism and mobility of dogma than those who meet us in the debate. However that may be – and I could be wrong about it – a genuine openness to the questions that another faith poses can mean, for the believer of any religion, a deeper entry into one's own faith. 'If,' said Father Yves Raguin at Chiang Mai, 'we have this humble attitude of one who is seeking for the real meaning of what he believes, and for the real face of the one in whom he believes, dialogue will be easy with the faithful of other religions.'

THE THINGS WE HAVE IN COMMON

I have said, paradoxically, that the primary common ground that we share in the dialogue is the sense of an absolute fidelity demanded of us towards certain convictions, even though the convictions themselves are irreconcilable. But besides that uncomfortable common factor there are a few other things which we do indubitably share.

We believe now that the Ultimate Reality upon which the faith of all believers is focused in every religion is the same, though our interpretations of his essential nature are still at variance.

The new interchange between men of different faiths has established the fact that all religions express an awareness of human alienation, enslavement, and need for healing and deliverance, and in all religions people experience an inward liberation, a sense of being accepted and made new.

Though the rituals of corporate and individual prayer differ widely, as does the degree of personalized encounter in the actual experience of prayer, yet the sense of oneness and communication with a gracious Divinity is common to them all, as is the hunger of the heart for such communion.

To be able to acknowledge this modest list of shared experiences is great gain, though the recognition of it raises as many questions as it answers. We are a long way from agreeing upon the meaning we may give to this common ground. And all the time the shadow of misapprehension falls between us. So I end, as I began, with my plea for patient persistence. We are, after all, only at the beginning of a new kind of exploration. When, as will often happen, we feel we are in the dark, we should not be ashamed to stand still rather than rush wildly forward.

> . . . Wait without hope,
> For hope would be hope for the wrong thing.
> Wait without love,
> For love would be love of the wrong thing.
> There is yet faith,
> But the faith and the hope and the love
> are all in the waiting . . .

CONTRIBUTORS AND ACKNOWLEDGEMENTS

ERNST TROELTSCH (1865–1923) was one of the leading German 'liberal Protestant' theologians of the early years of this century, and was associated with the well-known 'history of religions' school. He wrote influential essays on history, religion and theology, as well as a pioneering study in the sociology of religion, *The Social Teachings of the Christian Churches* (1912, English trans., London and New York, 1931).

'The Place of Christianity among the World Religions' was published in *Christian Thought: Its History and Application* (London, 1923), and shows his increasing sense of cultural relativism.

KARL BARTH (1886–1968), the Swiss Protestant theologian, was described by Pope Pius XII as the greatest theologian since Thomas Aquinas. His *The Epistle to the Romans* (2nd ed. 1921, English trans., London and New York, 1933) marked the beginnings of 'dialectical theology' and a sharp reaction against liberal theology. His unfinished *Church Dogmatics* represents the most thorough and uncompromising statement of Christian theology based solely on God's self-revelation in Jesus Christ.

'The Revelation of God as the Abolition of Religion' consists of extracts from *Church Dogmatics*, Vol. I, part 2 (English trans. 1956), section 17, and is reprinted by kind permission of the publishers, T. & T. Clark Ltd, of Edinburgh.

KARL RAHNER (b. 1904) is a member of the Society of Jesus and has been Professor of Dogmatic Theology at the universities of Innsbruck, Munich and Münster. One of the leading theologians of the Roman Catholic Church, he was a theological consultant at the Second Vatican Council. Many of his essays are being published in English in the volumes of *Theological Investigations* (London and New York, 1961–). His *Foundations of Christian Faith* appeared in 1976 (English trans., London and New York, 1978). It was Rahner who introduced the much-discussed notion of 'anonymous Christians'.

'Christianity and the Non-Christian Religions' is taken from *Theological Investigations*, Vol. V. (1966), and is reprinted by kind permission of the publishers, Darton, Longman and Todd Ltd, London, and Seabury Press Inc., New York.

The SECOND VATICAN COUNCIL, summoned by Pope John XXIII, met in four sessions from 1962 to 1964. It marked a turning point in the history of the Roman Catholic Church in the twentieth century. It initiated major changes in the Church's liturgy, and opened up new attitudes to other Christians, to other religions and to the secular world.

The English translation, by Thomas Athill, of the Council's 'Declaration on the Relation of the Church to Non-Christian Religions' is reprinted by kind permission of the Catholic Truth Society, London.

WILFRED CANTWELL SMITH (b. 1916) is Professor of the Comparative History of Religion at Harvard University. Having specialized, in early writings, on Islamic studies, he turned to the wider problem of world religion in a series of influential books, *The Meaning and End of Religion* (1962, reprinted New York and London, 1978), *Questions of Religious Truth* (London, 1967), *Belief and History* (Charlottesville, 1977), *Faith and Belief* (Princeton, 1979), *Towards a World Theology* (London, 1980). Cantwell Smith insists throughout his writings on the primacy of 'personal truth' over the truth of doctrines.

'The Christian in a Religiously Plural World' is taken from *Religious Diversity: Essays by Wilfred Cantwell Smith*, edited by Willard G. Oxtoby, published in 1976 by Harper and Row Inc., New York, and reprinted by kind permission of the publisher.

PAUL TILLICH (1886–1965) was one of the leading Protestant theologians of the twentieth century. Born in Germany, he began his university teaching in his native land, before emigrating to the United States in 1933. His chief works were written in English during his time as Professor of Philosophical Theology at Union Theological Seminary, New York. His

Systematic Theology appeared in three volumes between 1951 and 1963. In later life he moved to Chicago, where he worked in close conjunction with Mircea Eliade, the well-known historian of religion. Tillich came to speak of the spiritual reality in the depths of every living faith, yet he still considered the Cross of Christ to be the 'decisive' symbol in the history of religions.

'Christianity Judging Itself in the Light of its Encounter with the World Religions' is taken from the short book, *Christianity and the Encounter of the World Religions* (1963), the American Bampton Lectures, which Tillich delivered at Columbia University in 1961/2. He had been much influenced by his own encounter with Buddhism on a visit to Japan in 1960. The extract is reprinted by kind permission of the publishers, Columbia University Press, New York.

RAYMOND PANIKKAR (b. 1918), the son of a Hindu father and a Spanish Catholic mother, is a Roman Catholic priest, who has worked for many years in India, attempting to find and to show the meaning of Hindu philosophy for Christian self-understanding. In recent years he has taught in the United States and is now Professor of Religious Studies at the University of California in Santa Barbara. In 1977 he published a comprehensive interpretation of the basic Hindu scriptures, *The Vedic Experience* (London).

'The Unknown Christ of Hinduism', which illustrates the meeting of faiths in a less theoretical and more 'existential' way, is taken from the book of that title, published in 1968 by Darton, Longman and Todd, London, and reprinted by kind permission of the publisher.

STANLEY SAMARTHA (b. 1920) is the director of the Dialogue programme of the World Council of Churches, Geneva, Switzerland. He has edited many of the volumes of published papers from consultations organized by the World Council of Churches' sub-unit on Dialogue with People of Living Faiths and Ideologies.

'Dialogue as a Continuing Christian Concern' is taken from *Living Faiths and the Ecumenical Movement* (Geneva, 1971) and reprinted by kind permission of the author, who has contributed a further paragraph for this edition.

JOHN HICK (b. 1922) is H. G. Wood Professor of Theology at the University of Birmingham and Danforth Professor at the Claremont Graduate School of Religion, California. Well known for his writing on the philosophy of religion, particularly *Faith and Knowledge* (Ithaca and London, 1957) and *Evil and the God of Love* (London and New York, 1966), he has, in recent years, turned his attention to the problem of the conflicting truth claims of the different religions. His suggested 'Copernican revolution', whereby Christians are no longer to think of Christ at the centre, but of Christianity and the other faiths as all, in their different ways, mediating knowledge of the one God, has been widely discussed. These views were put forward in *God and the Universe of Faiths* (London and New York, 1973).

'Whatever Path Men Choose is Mine' was first published, in an earlier version, in *The Modern Churchman*, winter 1974, and is reprinted by kind permission of the editor.

JÜRGEN MOLTMANN (b. 1926) is one of the leading Protestant theologians in Germany. Since 1967 he has been Professor of Systematic Theology at Tübingen University. His theology of hope, involving a powerful reappraisal of New Testament eschatology and a marked political commitment, has been worked out in three books, *Theology of Hope* (English trans., London, 1967), *The Crucified God* (1974) and *The Church in the Power of the Spirit* (1977).

'Christianity and the World Religions' is taken from the last of these books, and is reprinted by kind permission of the publishers, SCM Press, London, and Harper and Row Inc., New York.

JOHN V. TAYLOR (b. 1914), author of *The Primal Vision: Christian Presence amid African Religion* (London, 1963) and *The Go-Between God: the Holy Spirit and the Christian Mission* (London, 1972), taught for many years in Africa before becoming General Secretary of the Church Missionary

Society. Now Bishop of Winchester, he is well known as an exponent of the idea of 'Christian presence'.

'The Theological Basis of Interfaith Dialogue' was delivered as the first Lambeth Interfaith Lecture on 2 November 1977 and is reprinted by kind permission of the author and of the Consultants to the Archbishops of Canterbury and York on Interfaith Relations.

The Editors are grateful to Dr Alan Keightley for assistance in reading the proofs.

BIBLIOGRAPHY

I. CHRISTIAN ATTITUDES TO OTHER RELIGIONS

E. L. Allen, *Christianity among the Religions.* Allen & Unwin, London, 1960

J. N. D. Anderson, *Christianity and Comparative Religion.* Tyndale Press, Wheaton, Illinois, 1970/Inter-Varsity Press, London, 1971

Karl Barth, *Church Dogmatics*, Vol. 1/2, section 17 (1939). T. & T. Clark, Edinburgh, 1956

A. C. Bouquet, *Is Christianity the Final Religion?* Macmillan, London, 1921

Emil Brunner, *Revelation and Reason*, SCM Press, London/Westminster Press, Philadelphia, 1947

Naomi Burton, ed. *The Asian Journal of Thomas Merton.* New Directions, New York, 1973/Sheldon Press, London, 1974

John B. Chethimattam, ed. *Unique and Universal.* Dharmaram College, Bangalore, 1972

William A. Christian, *Oppositions of Religious Doctrines.* Macmillan, London/Herder & Herder, New York, 1972

John B. Cobb, *The Structure of Christian Existence.* Westminster Press, Philadelphia, 1967/Lutterworth Press, London, 1968

Christ in a Pluralistic Age. Westminster Press, Philadelphia, 1975

Kenneth Cragg, *Christianity in World Perspective.* Lutterworth Press, London, 1968

The Christian and Other Religion. Mowbray, London, 1977

Charles Davis, *Christ and the World Religions.* Hodder & Stoughton, London, 1970

E. C. Dewick, *The Christian Attitude to Other Religions.* Cambridge University Press, 1953

John S. Dunne, *The Way of all the Earth.* Macmillan, New York/Collier Macmillan, London, 1972

James Dupuis, *Jesus Christ and His Spirit.* Theological Publications of India, Bangalore, 1977

Mircea Eliade & Joseph Kitagawa, eds. *Essays in Methodology.* University of Chicago Press, 1959

Essays on the Problem of Understanding. University of Chicago Press, 1968

H. H. Farmer, *Revelation and Religion.* Nisbet, London, 1954

Walter Freytag, *The Gospel and the Religions.* SCM Press, London, 1957

George Gispert-Sauch, ed. *God's Word among Men.* Vidyajoti, Delhi, 1973

Carl F. Hallencreutz, *Kraemer Towards Tambaram.* Uppsala, 1966

Dialogue and Community. World Council of Churches, Geneva, 1977

John Hick, *God and the Universe of Faiths.* Macmillan, London/St Martin's Press, New York, 1973. Paperback: Collins: Fount, Cleveland and London, 1977

ed. *Truth and Dialogue.* Sheldon Press, London/Westminster Press, Philadelphia, 1974

God Has Many Names. Macmillan, London, 1980

E. Hillman, *The Wider Ecumenism: Anonymous Christianity and the Church.* Burns & Oates, London/Herder & Herder, New York, 1968

W. E. Hocking, *Re-thinking Missions.* Harper & Row, New York, 1932

Living Religions and a World Faith. Allen & Unwin, London/Macmillan, New York, 1940

H. Jai Singh, ed. *Inter-Religious Dialogue.* Institute for the Study of Religion and Society, Bangalore, 1967

E. O. James, *Christianity and Other Religions.* Hodder & Stoughton, London, 1968

Hendrik Kraemer, *The Christian Message in a Non-Christian World.* Harper & Row, New York/Edinburgh House Press, London, 1938

Religion and the Christian Faith. Lutterworth Press, London, 1956

World Cultures and World Religions: The Coming Dialogue. Lutterworth Press, London, 1960

Why Christianity of all Religions? Lutterworth Press, London/Westminster Press, Philadelphia, 1962

Hans Küng, 'The World Religions in God's Plan of Salvation' in *Christian Revelation and World Religions*, ed. Joseph

Neuner. Burns & Oates, London, 1967

On Being A Christian, Part A, III. Doubleday, New York/Collins, London, 1976

A. T. van Leeuwen, *Christianity in World History*. Edinburgh House Press, London, 1964/Scribner's, New York, 1968

Stephen Neill, *Christian Faith and Other Faiths*. Oxford University Press, 1970

Joseph Neuner, ed. *Christian Revelation and World Religions*. Burns & Oates, London, 1967

Lesslie Newbigin, *The Finality of Christ*. SCM Press, London/John Knox Press, Atlanta, 1969

Raymond Panikkar, *The Unknown Christ of Hinduism*. Darton, Longman & Todd, London, 1964

The Trinity and the Religious Experience of Man. Darton, Longman & Todd, London, 1973

J. Pathrapankal, *Service and Salvation*. Theological Publications of India, Bangalore, 1973

E. Perry, *The Gospel in Dispute: the Relation of Christian Faith to Other Missionary Religions*. Doubleday, New York, 1958

Karl Rahner, 'Christianity and the Non-Christian Religions' in *Theological Investigations*, Vol. 5. Darton, Longman & Todd, London/Seabury Press, New York, 1966

'Reflections on Dialogue within a Pluralistic Society' in *Theological Investigations*, Vol. 6, 1969

'Anonymous Christianity and the Missionary Task of the Church' in *Theological Investigations*, Vol. 12, 1974

'Observations on the Problem of the "Anonymous Christian"' in *Theological Investigations*, Vol. 14, 1976

'Christ in Non-Christian Religions' in *God's Word among Men*, ed. G. Gispert-Sauch, Vidyajoti, Delhi, 1973

'Anonymous and Explicit Faith' and 'The One Christ and the Universality of Salvation' in *Theological Investigations*, Vol. 16, 1979

J. A. T. Robinson, *Truth is Two-Eyed*. SCM Press, London, 1979

H. R. Schlette, *Towards a Theology of Religions*. Burns & Oates, London, 1966

Albert Schweitzer, *Christianity and the Religions of the World*. Allen & Unwin, London, 1922/Holt, New York, 1939/Macmillan, London, 1951

Robert Lawson Slater, *Can Christians learn from Other Religions?* Seabury Press, New York, 1963

Ninian Smart, *World Religions: a Dialogue.* Pelican, London, 1960

'The Relation between Christianity and Other Religions' in *Soundings*, ed. A. R. Vidler. Cambridge University Press, 1962

Wilfred Cantwell Smith, *The Faith of Other Men* (1962). Harper Torchbooks, New York, 1972

The Meaning and End of Religion (1963). Harper & Row, New York/Sheldon Press, London, 1978

Questions of Religious Truth. Gollancz, London/Scribner's, New York, 1967

Religious Diversity, ed. W. G. Oxtoby. Harper & Row, New York, 1976

Towards a World Theology. Macmillan, London, 1980

H. van Straelen, *The Catholic Encounter with World Religions.* Burns & Oates, London/Newman Press, New York, 1966

M. M. Thomas, *Man and the Universe of Faiths.* Christian Literature Society, Madras, 1975

Owen C. Thomas, ed. *Attitudes Towards Other Religions.* SCM Press, London, 1969

Terry Thomas, *Inter-Religious Encounter.* Open University, Milton Keynes, 1978

Paul Tillich, *Christianity and the Encounter of the World Religions.* Columbia University Press, New York, 1963

The Future of Religions. Harper & Row, New York/Greenwood Press, London, 1966

Arnold Toynbee, *Christianity Among the Religions of the World.* Scribner's, New York, 1957

Ernst Troeltsch, *The Absoluteness of Christianity* (1901). John Knox Press, Atlanta, 1971/SCM Press, London, 1972

'The Place of Christianity among the World Religions' (1923) in *Christian Thought.* Meridian, New York/University of London Press, 1957

Ishanand Vempeny, *Inspiration in the Non-Biblical Scriptures.* Theological Publications of India, Bangalore, 1973

Max Warren, *I Believe in the Great Commission.* Hodder & Stoughton, London, 1976

R. C. Zaehner, *At Sundry Times.* Faber & Faber, London, 1958
The Convergent Spirit. Routledge & Kegan Paul, 1963/ *Matter and Spirit.* Harper & Row, New York, 1963
The Catholic Church and World Religions. Burns & Oates, London, 1964
The Concordant Discord. Oxford University Press, 1970

II. HISTORY OF CHRISTIAN ATTITUDES TO OTHER RELIGIONS

Carl F. Hallencreutz, *New Approaches to Men of Other Faiths.* World Council of Churches, Geneva, 1970
Dialogue and Community. World Council of Churches, Geneva, 1977
Eric J. Sharpe, *Not to Destroy but to Fulfil.* Gleerups, Lund, 1965
Comparative Religion: a History. Duckworth, London, 1975

III. CHRISTIANITY AND BUDDHISM

George Appleton, *On the Eightfold Path.* SCM Press, London, 1961
Hermann Beckh, *From Buddha to Christ.* Floris, Edinburgh, 1977
H. von Glasenapp, *Buddhism and Christianity.* Buddhist Publication Society, Kandy, 1963
Aelred Graham, *Conversations Christian and Buddhist.* Harcourt Brace, New York, 1971
William Johnston, *Silent Music.* Harper & Row, New York/ Collins, London, 1974
The Inner Eye of Love. Harper & Row, New York/Collins, London, 1978
Winston L. King, *Buddhism and Christianity.* Westminster Press, Philadelphia, 1962
William Peiris, *Edwin Arnold: His Life and Contribution to Buddhism.* Buddhist Publication Society, Kandy, 1970
Lynn A. de Silva, *The Problem of the Self in Buddhism and*

Christianity. Macmillan, London/Barnes & Noble, New York, 1979

B. H. Streeter, *The Buddha and the Christ*. Macmillan, New York, 1932

Towards the Meeting with Buddhism. Secretariat for Non-Christians, Rome, 1970

IV. CHRISTIANITY AND HINDUISM

Abhishiktananda (H. le Saux), *Prayer*. Indian SPCK, Delhi, 1967

Hindu-Christian Meeting Point. Christian Institute for the Study of Religion and Society, Bangalore, 1969

Guru and Disciple. SPCK, London, 1974

Saccidananda: A Christian Approach to Advaitic Experience. Indian SPCK, Delhi, 1974

The Further Shore. Indian SPCK, Delhi, 1975

Marcus Braybrooke, *Together to the Truth: Developments in Hindu and Christian Thought since 1800*. Indian SPCK, Delhi, 1971

John B. Chethimattam, *Patterns of Indian Thought*. Geoffrey Chapman, London/Orbis, Marynoll, 1971

J. N. Farquhar, *The Crown of Hinduism* (1913). Oxford University Press, 1930

M. K. Gandhi, *In Search of the Supreme*, ed. V. B. Kher, Vol. III, Section 7. Navajivan, Ahmedabad, 1962

S. K. George, *Gandhi's Challenge to Christianity*. Navajivan, Ahmedabad, 1947

Bede Griffiths, *Christian Ashram*. Darton, Longman & Todd, London, 1966

Christ in India. Scribner's, New York, 1967

Vedanta and Christian Faith. Dawn Horse Press, 1973

Return to the Centre. Collins, London/Templegate, New York, 1976. Paperback: Collins: Fount, London, 1978

A. G. Hogg, *The Christian Message to the Hindu*. SCM Press, London/Macmillan, New York, 1974

Karma and Redemption (1909). Christian Literature Society, Madras, 1970

Roger Hooker, *Journey into Varanasi*. Church Missionary Society, London, 1978

Klaus Klostermaier, *Hindu and Christian in Vrindaban*. SCM Press, London, 1969

S. Kulandran, *Grace in Christianity and Hinduism*. Lutterworth Press, London, 1964

J. Mattam, *Land of the Trinity: Modern Christian Approaches to Hinduism*. Theological Publications of India, Bangalore, 1975

Nirmal Minz, *Mahatma Gandhi and Hindu-Christian Dialogue*. Christian Literature Society, Madras, 1970

John Moffitt, *Journey to Gorakhpur*. Sheldon Press, London, 1973

Geoffrey Parrinder, *Avatar and Incarnation*. Faber & Faber, London, 1970

K. L. Seshagiri Rao, *Mahatma Gandhi and C. F. Andrews: A Study in Hindu-Christian Dialogue*. Punjabi University, 1969

Stanley Samartha, *The Hindu Response to the Unbound Christ*. Christian Literature Society, Madras, 1974

Eric Sharpe, *Faith Meets Faith: Some Christian Attitudes to Hinduism in the Nineteenth and Twentieth Centuries*. SCM Press, London, 1977

Ninian Smart, *The Yogi and the Devotee*. Allen & Unwin, London, 1968

M. M. Thomas, *The Acknowledged Christ of the Indian Renaissance*. SCM Press, London, 1969

V. CHRISTIANITY AND ISLAM

J. T. Addison, *The Christian Approach to the Moslem*. Columbia University Press, New York, 1942

T. Andrae, *Mohammed: the Man and his Faith*. Harper & Row, New York, 1955

Hasan Askari, *Inter-Religion*. Printwell Publications, Aligarh, 1977

J. L. Barton, *The Christian Approach to Islam*. Pilgrim Press, Boston, 1918

G. Bassetti-Sani, *Louis Massignon – Christian Ecumenist*. Franciscan Herald Press, Chicago, 1974

E. W. Bethmann, *Bridge to Islam*. Allen & Unwin, London, 1953

D. Brown, *Christianity and Islam* (5 vols). Sheldon Press, London, 1967–70: *Jesus and God*; *The Christian Scriptures*; *The Cross of the Messiah*; *The Divine Trinity*; *The Church and the Churches*

A New Threshold: Guidelines for the Churches in their Relations with Muslim Communities. British Council of Churches, London, 1976

The Way of the Prophet. Highway Press, London, 1962

L. E. Browne, *The Eclipse of Christianity in Asia.* Cambridge University Press, 1933

The Prospects of Islam. SCM Press, London, 1944

W. W. Cash, *Christendom and Islam: their contacts and cultures down the centuries.* SCM Press, London, 1937

J. Christiensen, *The Practical Approach to Muslims.* North Africa Mission, London, 1977

Kenneth Cragg, *The Call of the Minaret.* Oxford University Press, New York, 1965/Galaxy Books, Norfolk

ed. *Alive to God: Muslim and Christian Prayer.* Oxford University Press, 1970

The Dome and the Rock. SPCK, London, 1964

The Event of the Qur'an. Allen & Unwin, London, 1972

The House of Islam. Dickenson, Belmont, California, 1969

The Mind of the Qur'an. Allen & Unwin, London, 1973

The Privilege of Man. Athlone Press, London, 1968

Sandals at the Mosque. SCM Press, London, 1959

The Wisdom of the Sufis. Sheldon Press, London, 1976

trans. and Introduction, *The City of Wrong – a Friday in Jerusalem*, by M. K. Hussein. Seabury Press, New York, 1959

trans. and Introduction, *The Hallowed Valley – a Muslim Philosophy of Religion*, by M. K. Hussein.

trans. and Introduction, *Theology of Unity*, by Mohammed Abdul. Allen & Unwin, London, 1966

N. Daniel, *The Arabs and Medieval Europe.* Longman, London, 1979

Islam and the West: the Making of an Image. Edinburgh University Press, 1960

R. Frieling, *Christianity and Islam: a battle for the true image of man.* Floris Books, Edinburgh, 1978

T. Gairdner, *The Rebuke of Islam.* SPG, London, 1910

Guidelines for a Dialogue between Muslims and Christians.

Secretariat for Non-Christians, Rome, 1969
A. Guillaume, *Islam.* Penguin, London, 1954
E. Hahn, *Jesus in Islam: a Christian View.* Christian Centre, Krishnagiri, 1975
Muhammed, the Prophet of Islam. Henry Martyn Institute, Hyderabad, n.d.
Albert Hourani, *Western Attitudes Towards Islam.* Montefiore Memorial Lecture, Southampton University, 1974
J. Jomier, *The Bible and the Koran.* Desclée, New York, 1964
J. Kritzeck, *Peter the Venerable and Islam.* Princeton University Press, 1964
L. Levonian, *Studies in the Relationship between Islam and Christianity.* Allen & Unwin, London, 1940
D. B. Macdonald, *Aspects of Islam.* Macmillan, London, 1911
G. E. Marrison, *The Christian Approach to the Muslim.* Lutterworth Press, London, 1968
C. R. Marsh, *Share Your Faith with a Muslim.* Moody, Chicago, 1975
I. Maybaum, *Trialogue between Jew, Christian and Muslim.* Routledge & Kegan Paul, London, 1973
W. M. Miller, *A Christian Response to Islam.* Presbyterian & Reformed Publishing Co., USA, 1976
J. R. Mott, ed. *The Moslem World Today.* Hodder & Stoughton, London, 1925
W. Muir, trans. *The Apology of al-Kindi* (Christian-Muslim Dialogue). SPCK, London, 1911
C. Padwick, *Muslim Devotions.* SPCK, London, 1961
Temple Gairdner of Cairo. SPCK, London, 1930
G. Parrinder, *Jesus in the Qur'an.* Sheldon Press, London, 1976
D. Rahbar, *The God of Justice.* E. J. Brill, Leiden, 1960
D. J. Sahas, *John of Damascus on Islam.* E. J. Brill, Leiden, 1972
Stanley Samartha and John B. Taylor, eds, *Christian-Muslim Dialogue* (Broumana Consultation, 1972). World Council of Churches, Geneva, 1973.
F. Schuon, *Understanding Islam.* Allen & Unwin, London, 1965
Dimensions of Islam. Allen & Unwin, London, 1970
P. Seale, *Qur'an and Bible.* Croom Helm, London, 1978
W. C. Smith, *Islam in Modern History.* Mentor Books, New

York, 1959/London, 1965

R. W. Southern, *Western Views of Islam in the Middle Ages.* Harvard University Press, 1962

H. Spencer, *Islam and the Gospel of God: a comparison of the central doctrines of Christianity and Islam.* SPCK, London, 1956

J. W. Sweetman, *Islam and Christian Theology* (4 vols). Lutterworth Press, London, 1945–67

W. M. Watt, *Muhammad: Prophet and Statesman.* Oxford University Press, 1961

Islamic Revelation. Edinburgh University Press, 1969

Truth in the Religions. Edinburgh University Press, 1963

C. V. Werff, *Christian Mission to Muslims – the Record.* William Carey Library, Pasadena, 1977

Christians Meeting Muslims: Ten Years of Christian-Muslim Dialogue. World Council of Churches, Geneva, 1977

S. M. Zwemer, *Islam – a Challenge to Faith.* New York, 1907

The Moslem Christ. London, 1915

Raymond Lull: first missionary to the Moslems. New York, 1902

VI. CHRISTIANITY AND JUDAISM

Leo Baeck, *Judaism and Christianity.* Jewish Publication Society of America, 1958/Harper Torchbooks, New York, 1966

Paul Borchsenius, *Two Ways to God.* Valentine, Mitchell, New York, 1968

A. Roy Eckhardt, *Elder and Younger Brothers: the Encounter of Jews and Christians.* Scribner's, New York, 1967

Charles Glock and Rodney Stark, *Christian Beliefs and Anti-Semitism.* Harper & Row, New York, 1966

Walter Jacob, *Christianity Through Jewish Eyes.* Hebrew Union College Press, New York, 1974

Jewish-Christian Dialogue. World Council of Churches, Geneva, 1975

Jacob Katz, *Exclusiveness and Tolerance.* Schocken, New York, 1975

Charlotte Klein, *Anti-Judaism in Christian Theology.* Fortress Press, Philadelphia/SPCK, London, 1978

Hans Küng and Pinchas Lapide, *Brother or Lord?* Collins: Fount, London/Doubleday, New York, 1977

I. Maybaum, *Trialogue between Jew, Christian and Muslim.* Routledge & Kegan Paul, London, 1973

James Parkes, *Prelude to Dialogue.* Valentine, Mitchell, New York, 1969

The Conflict of the Church and the Synagogue. Atheneum, New York, 1969

John D. Rayner, *Towards Mutual Understanding.* James Clarke, London, 1960

F. Rosenweig, *The Star of Redemption.* Routledge & Kegan Paul, London, 1971

Samuel Sandmel, *We Jews and You Christians.* Lippincott, New York, 1967

The Genius of Paul. Fortress Press, Philadelphia, 1970

A Jewish Understanding of the New Testament. SPCK, London, 1977

Judaism and Christian Beginnings. Oxford University Press, 1978

Anti-Semitism in the New Testament? Fortress Press, Philadelphia, 1978

Peter Schneider, *Sweeter than Honey.* SCM Press, London, 1966/*The Dialogue of Christians and Jews.* Seabury Press, New York, 1967

Trude Weiss-Rosmarin, *Judaism and Christianity: the Differences.* Jonathan David, 1972

VII. CHRISTIANITY AND THE PRIMAL RELIGIONS

Kwesi Dickson and Paul Ellingworth, eds, *Biblical Revelation and African Beliefs.* Lutterworth Press, London, 1969

Bengt Sundkler, *The Christian Ministry in Africa.* SCM Press, London, 1960

John V. Taylor, *The Primal Vision: Christian Presence and African Religion.* SCM Press, London/Fortress Press, Philadelphia, 1963

ed. *Primal World Views: Christian Dialogue with Traditional Thought.* Daystar Press, Ibadan, 1976

D. Westermann, *Africa and Christianity*. Oxford University Press, 1937

VIII. THE ECUMENICAL MISSIONARY MOVEMENT AND THE WORLD COUNCIL OF CHURCHES

World Missionary Conference, 1910, 10 vols. Oliphant, Anderson and Ferrier, London, 1910

International Missionary Council, Jerusalem Conference, 1928. Oxford University Press, 1928

International Missionary Council, Tambaram (Madras) Conference, 1938, 7 vols. Oxford University Press, 1939

Norman Goodall, ed. *Missions Under the Cross* (IMC, Willingen, 1952). International Missionary Council, London, 1953

Ronald Orchard, ed. *International Missionary Council, Ghana, 1958*. Edinburgh House Press, London, 1958

Ronald Orchard, ed. *Witness in Six Continents* (WCC Commission on World Mission & Evangelism, Mexico City, 1963). Edinburgh House Press, London, 1964

Stanley Samartha, ed. *Dialogue Between Men of Living Faiths* (Ajaltoun, 1970). World Council of Churches, Geneva, 1971

Living Faiths and the Ecumenical Movement. World Council of Churches, Geneva, 1971

Pauline Webb, *Salvation Today* (Bangkok, 1973). SCM Press, London, 1974

Stanley Samartha, ed. *Towards World Community* (Colombo, 1974). World Council of Churches, Geneva, 1975

Dialogue in Community (Chiang Mai, 1977). World Council of Churches, Geneva, 1977

Guidelines on Dialogue with People of Living Faiths and Ideologies. World Council of Churches, Geneva, 1979

IX. NON-CHRISTIAN VIEWS OF CHRISTIANITY

Moses Jung, Swami Nikhilananda and Herbert Schneider, eds, *Relations among Religions Today*. E. J. Brill, Leiden, 1963

David W. McKain, ed. *Christianity: Some non-Christian Approaches*. Greenwood Press, London, 1964

INDEX